Photographs by Michael W Richards (RSPB)

Bempton Cliffs

£1.95

SBN 361 03905 0
Copyright © 1977 Purnell and Sons Limited
Published 1977 by Purnell Books, Berkshire House, Queen Street,
Maidenhead. Berkshire
Made and printed in Great Britain by Purnell and Sons Limited,
Paulton (Bristol) and London

Compiled by Linda Bennett and Sylvia Sullivan

The great thing about birds is that you can watch them virtually anywhere and at any time. You can never be sure what you are going to see, but there's bound to be some interesting behaviour or an unusual species to watch.

Recently I drove along the M6 to a YOC meeting in Cumbria. Some people say that motorway driving is dull, but on this occasion I not only saw the usual kestrels hunting over the verges, rooks searching along the hard shoulder and lapwings flying overhead, but also a buzzard which flew round in a leisurely fashion, and a heron which stood on the side of the road, showing no fear as my car passed within a metre or two. These, plus the other more usual birds, meant that I had seen 15 species on one motorway journey.

Then there's the discovery of the unexpected. I can see no attraction in searching for rare birds that other birdwatchers have found and it is better for the birds if they are left alone. But finding an unexpected species in your own patch is a great thrill.

I vividly remember a warm September evening when I visited a local gravel pit that I had been watching regularly during the summer. Sand martins were busy feeding over the water, ducks were flying in to roost and grebes silently diving for fish. Suddenly a larger bird appeared among the martins. Its short tail and pointed wings told me it was a hobby. The falcon tried to grab a sand martin but missed. Then it flew up over my head, circled round and came in low for a second attempt. This time it was successful and, clutching the sand martin in its talons, flew to a post in a nearby field where it started to pluck its prey. Fantastic!—the whole drama took place within a few metres of where I sat—and it was the first hobby I'd ever seen!

Watch any area for long enough and you too will see a surprising number of different species.

Wherever you live there will be plenty of birds for you to study and exciting discoveries to make. Remember, if you join the YOC you will be able to report your observations and take part in national surveys which we organise. So if you are not already a member, turn to page 77 and join us now!

Peter Holden
YOC National Organiser

RSPB YOC
BIRD LIFE annual

Purnell

Michael W Richards (RSPB)

Goldfinch

A sure way of attracting birds is to provide them with water. Next to food, there is nothing they like more than water, for drinking and bathing.

When photographer Ernest Janes set out to take shots of woodland birds, he picked an area rich in wildlife but with no natural water supplies. So he turned landscape gardener.

He sank a fibreglass pond, three feet in diameter and five inches deep, in the heart of a 120-acre Hertfordshire wood. He turfed the edges and allowed spring vegetation to complete the important job of camouflage round the pool and his hide.

A perch was angled gently into the water to give bathtime visitors a chance to test the depth before taking the plunge.

The only problem was that most of the water had to be transported two miles from home and then half a mile on foot into the wood. Ernest estimates that he humped something like 14 gallons a week to keep the pool topped up. "But it was well worth the effort," he said. Thirty-three different species became regular visitors to his woodland oasis.

Female blackcap

Woodland Oasis

Chaffinch and great tit

Great tit

Male chaffinch
G St J Hollis

Rest in Peace

I pass through Norwich Cemetery on my way to school, and although some would not relish the prospect, I, on the contrary, actually look forward to my daily trip. For I have found the quiet and peace has made the area a sanctuary for hundreds of birds, and every day I see both new and familiar faces.

As the winter begins, I stop for a few moments each day to throw a handful of seeds and scraps to the ever-hungry population. A robin quickly becomes tame enough to feed from my outstretched hand. A collection of tits and finches eagerly await my arrival. Flocks of bramblings and chaffinches forage for food undisturbed, while redwings and fieldfares are tame enough to feed only a few yards away from my feet.

Flocks of starlings soon move in and one corner which is littered with white droppings is often used as a collecting point before the birds move off to their evening roost.

Black-headed gulls scream overhead, appearing as if from nowhere at the first hint of food. Blackbirds find the fresh-turned earth from a new grave brings worms to the surface.

The spring term—and now birds are courting, inspecting nest-sites, building, laying and finally rearing their young. Bullfinches, with their distinctive "heavy" outline, strip the ornamental flowering cherries, nipping out the soft buds. Then the swallows arrive and with them the cuckoos, whose melodious, two-tone call blends with the soft cooings of the wood

pigeons. Nuthatches and treecreepers scurry up and down the sheer trunks; goldcrests and coal tits feed high in the conifers. A spotted flycatcher darts out at a passing fly, twisting and turning but seldom missing. An occasional linnet perches on a grave-stone, wrens hop from branch to branch in the shrub borders while below a dunnock searches for insects.

As summer turns to autumn the bird life slowly fades, although I have seen some of my best birds in this season. One November morning a large, brown bird with distinctive eye-stripes and barred flanks dashed out of the fog across my path and swerved away—my first and only red-legged partridge. A jay, too, usually only a harsh shriek and a flash of blue among the trees, suddenly started making morning appearances at my feeding place, and became surprisingly tame before suddenly and mysteriously disappearing one day.

So the year turns full cycle. Long may I tread the familiar paths; long may the birds rest there—in peace.

8

● **by Fenella Smith** (YOC Member)

Identifying Terns

Terns are graceful, stream-lined birds with long wings and forked tails; they are sometimes rather aptly called sea swallows. All the species that regularly breed in the British Isles have jet-black caps, silver-grey backs and lighter underparts, so identification can pose problems. But look for the bill colour and listen for the different calls.

Terns catch their food, small fish and sand eels, by hovering high above the surface of the water and plunging straight down at any likely prey. They are only summer visitors to Britain, arriving from their warmer winter quarters round the African coast during April. The Arctic tern is one of our greatest wanderers, returning in the autumn to the Antarctic reg-ions; its twice-yearly journey may be as long as 11,000 miles.

Common tern

Black-tipped red bill helps to distinguish the common tern from the Arctic tern. The common tern is the most widely distributed of our British terns and nests in large, noisy colonies which are found inland as well as on the coast.

Because the two species are difficult to separate in the field, birdwatchers often refer to birds they cannot be sure of as "comic terns".

During the 19th century terns, like many other seabirds, were persecuted by egg-collectors for food and sport. However, the introduction of a Seabirds Protec-tion Bill in 1896 helped to brighten their prospects. Today more than 10,000 pairs of common terns nest in Britain and Ireland, and on the RSPB reserves of Minsmere and Havergate in Suffolk, Dungeness in Kent and Snettisham in Norfolk they have been encouraged to nest on specially constructed shingle islands.

Arctic tern

The Arctic tern, unlike the common tern, has a pure red bill and grey, translucent-looking underwings; the tail streamers are also longer.

The Arctic tern is the most numerous tern in Britain—its breeding population numbers about 40,000 pairs, and the col-onies are always near the coast. It is a more northern bird than the common tern, Britain being the very south of its breeding range.

Arctic terns are extremely aggressive when on their breeding grounds and will actually attack intruding birdwatchers.

Sandwich tern

The largest of our nesting terns, the Sandwich tern is rather thinner and more angular in shape than the common or Arctic tern, with a shorter tail. Also, the black cap of the adult is rather shaggy at the back and can be raised like a crest when the bird is excited. Its call is a rasping "kirrik" and it is among the noisiest of our terns, often nesting in mixed colonies alongside common and Arctic terns and black-headed gulls.

About 12,000 pairs nest in Britain and Ireland but this number can vary considerably from year to year—if these birds are disturbed during egg-laying the whole colony may desert. In 1974 Sandwich terns breeding on the RSPB reserve at Minsmere were disturbed by a fox and the whole colony left the reserve. Eventually, a few pairs attempted to breed on the neighbouring reserve of Havergate—at least the birds showed a preference for RSPB reserves!

Roseate tern

The roseate tern, with its red-tipped black bill and pale rose-tinted breast in the spring, is the rarest breeding seabird in Britain and Ireland. In 1974 about 1400 pairs nested in a handful of scat-tered colonies round our coasts, their numbers having slowly declined since 1950. The reason for the decrease is not known, but these birds are trapped in Ghana, West Africa, for food. As this is one of the birds' main wintering areas, it is possible that this slaughter is affecting their numbers.

Little tern

The little tern, as its name suggests, is the smallest British tern. It has a typical pale grey back and white underparts, but its black cap is incomplete at the front; its bill is yellow with a black tip.

Between 1600 and 1800 pairs breed round our coasts on shingle and sand beaches. Little tern col-onies are threatened with many dangers—high tides can wash away nests and strong winds can completely bury the eggs. As if this were not enough, holidaymakers can accidentally walk on the beaut-ifully camouflaged eggs or keep the adult away from the nest for long periods of time. In certain areas the RSPB has roped or wired off the nesting sites and summer wardens look after the birds for the crucial nesting period.

Black tern

The black tern, unlike the five sea terns just described, is a marsh tern, preferring to nest inland near lakes or rivers. It does not breed regularly in Britain and Ireland (the numbers that have attempted to breed can be counted on the fingers of one hand), but is a com-mon visitor during the spring and autumn migrations.

ARCTIC TERN

British

ROSEATE TERN

COMMON
TERN
Winter

COMMON TERN Summer

Terns

SANDWICH TERN

BLACK TERN Winter

BLACK TERN Summer

LITTLE TERN

A Birdwatcher's Calendar

JANUARY

Put up a bird table in your garden and feed the birds regularly during cold weather.

Garden birds need plenty of food and water during the cold days.

Look out for lapwings moving south-west in cold weather.

FEBRUARY

Make and erect nestboxes in your garden. Instructions sent on receipt of a stamped addressed envelope at YOC headquarters.

Some birds start to sing from regular posts declaring their territories.

During the mild days rooks return to their rookeries and start building or repairing their nests.

A good time for looking at wildfowl on reservoirs.

MARCH

Keep a sharp look-out for the first summer migrants to arrive.

Great crested grebes begin their courtship displays.

Flocks of small birds move through the countryside. Soon they will be setting up their territories for the spring.

Broods of ducklings may be seen at the end of the month.

APRIL

Stop feeding garden birds—unnatural food may be harmful to young birds.

Summer migrants are arriving or passing through to their breeding grounds further north.

Many birds are busy building nests.
Cock wrens build several before the female chooses one.

MAY

Don't rescue young birds —leave it to the parents to do the job.
Plan your summer holiday and write off for permits if you want to visit RSPB reserves.

Dawn chorus is at its height—even before the sun rises.

Many young birds out of their nests, while other birds are still building nests or incubating eggs.

JUNE

An ideal time to be a nature detective. Find out which birds nest in your area by looking for broken egg shells, young birds or adult birds carrying food.

First signs of autumn as lapwings and lesser black-backed gulls return from their breeding grounds.

A busy month with more young birds to be seen. Many species, like blackbirds, are now raising a second brood.

July to December appears on pages 70 and 71

The chough is symbolic of wild and rugged coasts bordering the Atlantic. The late James Fisher, a famous ornithologist, named it "The air-acrobat of the western cliffs". Its chosen nest-sites have been used by generations of choughs who, apparently, never move more than a few miles away to feed or roost.

Despite its brave and cheerful way, there is a certain melancholy about this bird. For reasons only guessed at, its numbers have decreased over the past hundred years or so. In Cornwall it was claimed as the "Cornish chough" so well-known was it in that county. But now it is no longer seen there.

Today, it survives along stretches of sea-cliffs in Ireland —the stronghold—and in isolated groups in SW Scotland and Wales. A few pairs still cling on in the mountains of Snowdonia where it nests in mine-shafts and disused quarries.

If you know where to look for choughs, the bird will first call attention to itself with its high-pitched, ringing "chee-ow". Then a dark, jackdaw-sized shape will slant swiftly into view, call again, and dive below the cliff to wave level, and, light as a feather, shoot up again. A second bird will follow a few metres behind giving an identical performance. This is how a pair of choughs go on, never out of sight or sound of each other. It's widely held that when the young choose their mates in autumn it most certainly means "from this day forward 'til death do us part". In the breeding season, ravens, crows and jackdaws share the cliffs, making identification difficult. The chough is a more compact shape than the rest with broad wings and squared-off tail. The wing primaries are widely splayed, but this is not always easy to see. It is the buoyant flight and two-syllabled call which singles out the chough.

With young about, the birds are surprisingly tame, shouting defiantly from a nearby rock. With each call, the head is dipped and wings flicked upwards. Such close-up views reveal the chough's ele-

● by Susan Cowdy—Naturalist and RSPB council member

14

The Air~acrobat
of the cliffs

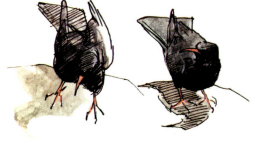

gance: the shining black plumage, iridescent with green, blue and purple; coral-coloured bill curving to a forcep tip; strong, bright red legs and eyes of darkest brown. The bird stands proud, head held high with a haughty air.

The haunt of the chough is where many of us yearn to be in the distracting months of May and June: a western isle with daunting cliffs topped by slippery grass slopes; the heavy swell of a recent gale breathing in and out far below, where razorbills float like toys on the sun-green surface of the sea.

In the roof of a cavern just below, the birds have built a nest of heather stalks, softly lined with sheep's wool. Bringing wool to the nest is a ritual performed by the hen bird. What happens if there are no sheep on the island? Rabbits' fur is never substituted. One nest on a sheepless island off Ireland was found to be lined from the softest plant available, sea campion. Choughs on the Calf of Man were watched collecting wool from

the Isle of Man, three miles across the sea. It took the birds about a dozen round trips of 20 minutes each to collect sufficient wool. On all the journeys, the male accompanied his mate empty-billed, except on one return trip when he brought back one small wad of wool.

The female starts brooding when the first egg is laid. The male brings her food to the nest until the young are hatched. The nestlings are fed by both parents and after a month are strong enough to come to the entrance of the cavern to demand food. They are fed almost entirely with regurgitated ants and their larvae, brought to them in the parents' crop at 20-minute intervals. As the young grow, they seem to know when the time for the parent birds' return is at hand, and squawk loudly in their dark recess.

After delivering the meal the parents spend some time cleaning themselves up. First, they wipe their bills with great knife-

sharpening swipes against the rock face. Their face feathers become wet and matted from the task of forcing the food down the throats of their young. These feathers are scratched feverishly as if to remove some irritating substance, perhaps formic acid from the ants which form the main part of the diet in spring. A typical scratching movement is performed by dropping a wing and lifting a leg over the carpel joint allowing precise scratching round nostrils and eyes.

It is fascinating to watch the pair "allopreen" by gently nibbling round each other's head feathers.

The day comes when the fledglings are considered old enough to fly. They are called from their hiding holes around the nest-site, encouraged to be brave and follow their parents who, at first, make short demonstration flights. First shaky attempts are made over short distances, later they follow above the sea and along the cliff. At this age, the young look rather like overgrown starlings, with short straw-coloured bills and

Illustrations by John Busby

15

light coloured legs. Within three weeks they have grown so fast that in flight it is difficult to tell young from old.

There is apparently no animosity between choughs and jackdaws. Jackdaws use different nest-sites and feed on different food. The only bird which frightens the chough is the hunting peregrine. In fact, except for man, choughs have no enemies; they nest out of reach of rats and foxes. Even so, some years ago tragedy hit the Bardsey Island choughs. One spring, a pair were seen sitting disconsolately near their cave. The nest lining had been dragged out and hung in strands from the entrance; the nestlings had disappeared, obviously removed by force. The culprit was never proved, but little owls suspected as they were known to drag unfortunate Manx shearwater chicks from their burrows.

Although the chough has declined in numbers and its range has become restricted from what it was a hundred years ago, perhaps the recent mild winters in Wales have helped, as some ancient nest-sites have been recolonised. So, for the moment, the red-billed chough hangs on. A specialised feeder, living in comparative isolation for parts of the year, surviving appalling winter storms with lashing seas. But this is the way of the chough, who prefers to live in the words of the Irish poet with:

"Sea, the earth, the skies,
The blowing of the winds,
Where there is loneliness in
all of them together."

Think twice before you buy a pet bird. For every wild bird that reaches the bird-keeper at least two more have died somewhere on their long journey.

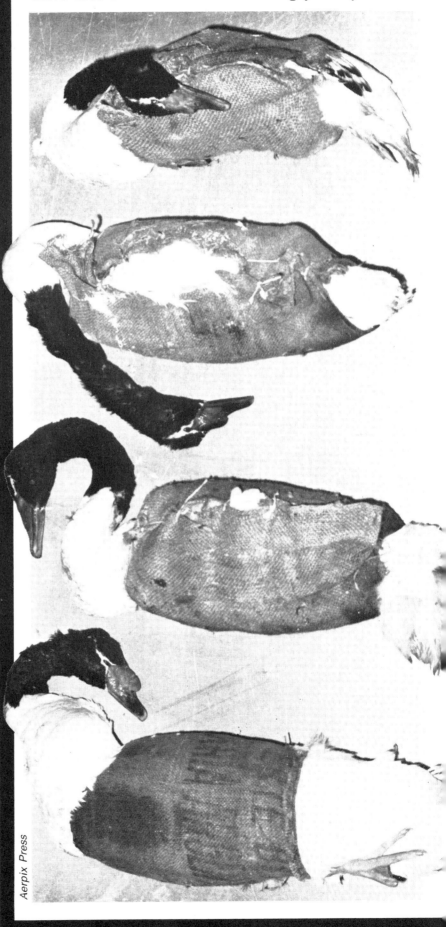

Aerpix Press

16

Airborne Birds

Wild birds are trapped widely in Asia, Africa and South America. Snares, twigs covered with a sticky substance called bird lime, traps and nets are all used. Many die at this stage and those that survive are taken to a local collecting centre, during which journey as many as half may die from shock, starvation or overcrowding. Then comes another journey—this time to an exporting depot, where they are kept until enough are collected to make up a large consignment for export.

Export is usually by air and, although there are international regulations governing the transport of birds by air, the conditions in which many airlines allow their bird cargoes to be transported are disgusting. The regulations state the numbers of birds that may be carried and the sort of cage each species should be put in, but when Tim Inskipp, an RSPB researcher, looked at the conditions under which birds arrived at London's Heathrow Airport during 1976 he could find no cages that complied with the **Live Animal Regulations.**

Most horrifying of the examples of overcrowding was a consignment of 2120 birds from India, of which 2029 were dead on arrival. This meant that 95.7 per cent of the birds died and in some of the cages there were 45 times as many parrots as there should have been according to the regulations. In this case the airline concerned was fined over £3000, but it was no isolated incident; in two years there were 23 incidents of consignments of birds in which more than 16 per cent of the birds were dead on arrival.

Overcrowding means stress for the birds; they cannot reach their food or water and are liable to fight each other. In the past there

Dead black-necked swans from Argentina, part of a consignment crammed into boxes with no food or water.

Peregrine falcon sent from India with a live pigeon for food.

Aerpix Press

have been astounding examples of ignorance on the part of the exporter. One cage containing a peregrine falcon and a crested hawk eagle also contained two live pigeons, presumably put in as food. On arrival the falcon and hawk eagle and one pigeon were alive. The other pigeon was dead, having been accidentally squashed. What the exporter had not realised was that birds of prey catch their prey in flight and will ignore the pigeons.

The world trade in birds affects at least $5\frac{1}{2}$ million birds. The British Isles alone import more than 600,000 birds each year. When these figures were first published in the RSPB's report *All Heaven in a Rage* in 1975, aviculturists, conservationists and government officials were surprised. Questions were asked in the Houses of Parliament and government departments reacted swiftly. Quarantine restrictions were placed on imported birds and the Government promised to restrict ports and airports through which animals could be imported and to set up reception centres at these ports.

In the research that went into this report it became obvious that there was little known about the conditions under which the birds travelled. So Tim Inskipp undertook another study to find out whether the **Live Animal Regulations** drawn up by the International Air Travel Association were being adhered to. During this investigation he examined over 800 cages in detail and found none that fulfilled all aspects of the regulations.

The RSPB is convinced that the situation could be improved. So are a number of members of parliament, civil servants, airport officials and the RSPCA. Public opinion is becoming so strong that we are all sure that steps must be taken to ensure that the way we treat captive birds is improved.

Much of the problem would disappear if more were done to breed birds in captivity. Some species breed easily and these are the ones to go for if you want to keep a bird yourself. Canaries and budgerigars are excellent species to keep. All have been bred in captivity and they live for quite a long time. Attractive as they may be, many species that have been taken from the wild will probably not survive for long in a cage.

1

2

Birdtable
Birds

3

Here are some of the birds you might find coming to your bird-table. You are sure to see certain members of the tit family—coal tits and great tits (fig 1) or blue tits feeding from a coconut (2). The great spotted woodpecker (3) would be a rather more unusual visitor and jays (4) are normally shy, woodland birds. Bird-tables provide an excellent opportunity for watching birds, like the blue tit (5) demonstrating his acrobatic expertise, and the great tit (6) showing his beautiful bold markings.

4

5

On the next page there are instructions for making your own bird-table.

6

19

Make a Birdtable

One sure way of attracting birds to your garden is to provide a well-stocked birdtable. Birdtables come in all shapes and sizes and can be bought from the RSPB, but here are instructions for making your own birdtable.

You will need a piece of exterior quality plywood, about 30 cm×46 cm and 1 cm thick. You will then need a wooden batten a centimetre squared by about 1½ metres long. Cut the batten to four lengths —two of 26 cm and two of 46 cm, then screw or nail these to each side of the table, leaving a gap at each corner. This will prevent the food being blown away and yet allow water to drain off.

A few hooks screwed into the wooden battens would be useful for hanging chop bones, strings of peanuts and a food basket.

The next step is to screw one small screw-eye into the battens at each corner of the table. Then attach two lengths of terylene or nylon cord (about 60 cm long) to the eyes and tie them to a branch of the tree you wish to hang the table from. Alternatively you can fix your table to a post using four metal angle brackets.

You can put out a wide variety of foods, including peanuts, sultanas and fresh (not desiccated) coconut. Nearly all kitchen scraps are suitable—stale cake, bread

(preferably brown), potatoes, apple cores, chopped bacon rind, suet, fat, meat bones and cheese. Mealworms and packets of seed foods can be bought from petshops, although you may like to collect sunflower seeds and nuts such as beechmast, yourself.

It is not necessary to feed birds in spring and summer when there is plenty of natural food about, and in fact it may even be a bad thing as the parents may not provide the right diet for their young. However, water is important for birds all the year round. Now turn to page 42 for details of how to make your own garden pond.

The Disappearing Ibis

In this article Richard Porter, who has been studying Turkish birds for over ten years, looks at one whose future is not very bright—the bald ibis. It is one of the rarest birds in the world.

On a white cliff face rising from the middle of a small Asian town is a colony of one of the world's rarest birds. The town is Birecik. It stands beside the upper Euphrates, which flows through rolling agricultural land of wheat, hemp and pistachios amidst the bleached hills and eroded ravines of south-east Turkey. The bird is the bald ibis.

In the sixteenth century, when Birecik was a dockyard town that built the Tigris and Euphrates river boats, one could have described other colonies from the Swiss Alps, the Danube, or the Rhone, where remains of this bird have been found. Once, apparently, the ibis was widespread in Europe, western Asia, and North Africa, but now, alas, it is confined to only Morocco and this one small town in Turkey. In 1975 a survey showed that the world breeding population was about 275 pairs, of which just 25 were at Birecik.

I saw the Birecik colony in 1970. My feeling then was one of being lulled back to biblical times as the muddy river washed against its sandy banks, overlooked by flat-topped and half-constructed mud-baked houses that formed a contrasting pattern with the harsh shadows of the dazzling Asian sunlight.

Bare-footed children, donkeys, and palm doves all seemed to have equal status amongst the cobbled streets. The ibises, with their glossy black plumage, red vulturine heads, long curved bills, and mystical calls, could, like the townsfolk themselves, have been lifted from a scene in Exodus.

To the villagers of Birecik the bald ibis has always been a sacred bird. Its arrival in the spring, remarkably consistent on 14 February, was in days gone by an anniversary of the annual floods. There were celebrations and sheep sacrifices, but with the arrival of immigrant people from Syria and Kurdistan this ancient custom lost its verve.

We do not know how large this ibis colony was in those earlier times. Perhaps it did not exist, for the botanist Leonhard Rauwolf did not mention it when he crossed the Euphrates at Birecik in 1574, bound for his adventures in India. The earliest record that we have of this ibis population dates from 1953, when there were about 530 pairs. In 1970 there were about 36.

The large "mud and wattle" nests are crammed on a single ledge of the small cliff in the centre of the town. A few more pairs are scattered on the cliffs that overhang a cement works at the water's edge.

What are the reasons for the decline? Though its diet has been little studied, the bird has a reputation for devouring large quantities of grasshoppers and also takes fish and worms. A number of insect-killing chemicals are used by the farmers in the area, but are these having any effect? In 1972 a party from the World Wildlife Fund took an unhatched egg and brought it back to England for analysis. It was found to contain a small amount of these chemicals —too small to be harmful.

More work needs to be done on this bird's feeding ecology. We also need to know what happens when the ibis migrates south in autumn. What threats does it face in its wintering area, which is thought to be in the highlands of Ethiopia? Bald ibises are seen here regularly in winter but there is some uncertainty whether these are from the Moroccan colony or Birecik. Ringing or marking the birds would provide the answer.

Another possible reason for the decline is that although ibises have apparently tolerated people and their buildings for many decades, they are being put under increasing pressure as the population of Birecik grows and more houses are erected against and above the cliff face. But if this is the reason, why hasn't the bird colonised any of the other cliffs along the upper Euphrates?

Anxious to help the disappearing ibis, the World Wildlife Fund in 1973 launched a project to save the population at Birecik which had dropped to just 26 pairs. A German scientist, Udo Hirsch, was put in charge and every encouragement was provided by Tansu Gurpinar and Belkis and Salih Acar, eminent Turkish conservationists. He studied the breeding and feeding behaviour, revived amongst the townsfolk the ancient festival to welcome the ibises in spring, and built artificial wooden platforms to increase the ledges available for nesting. The efforts were well rewarded for 22 young flew from the 26 pairs, whereas in each of the previous

two years no more than 11 young had flown.

Since 1973 the Turks themselves have helped warden the area, and there have even been plans to buy some of the houses on the cliff face, knock them down and thus free the area for colonisation by the ibises. This continued protection appears to have helped, for in 1975, though the number of pairs was about the same (25 to be precise), the young produced had increased to 36.

I wish them well, but as my mind wanders back to those parched summer days and recalls the lament in the harsh, mournful calls of a small flock circling over the town in the warm air thermals, black against vivid blue, I try to imagine their long journey in autumn to the high ranges of Ethiopia and feel sadly that the bald ibis is rapidly passing into history. I hope I am wrong.

By the end of the summer of 1973, 26 pairs had nested and young were reared. In 1974, 25 pairs reared about 60 young, and in 1975 25 pairs reared 36 young.

Udo Hirsch

Outlook

At YOC headquarters we are always pleased to hear from members and in every issue of *Bird Life* there is a page or two devoted to their own observations. Here is a selection of some of the special notes which have appeared in the magazine in recent years . . .

A fishy story

One day in December I was sitting in a tree at the edge of the River Mole hoping to watch two herons which had just moved into the area. I sat for some time without seeing them. Suddenly, my attention was drawn to a small, brown bird foraging in the debris at the side of a large pool which had been left after flooding. The bird was a wren. Then, without warning, the small bird hurled itself at the edge of the pool and to my astonishment pulled out a small fish about a centimetre long. After beating the fish four or five times against the bank it devoured it greedily, then went on foraging in the debris.

Terry Pullinger

Wrens have been observed foraging in shallow streams to take caddisfly larvae, tadpoles, minnows and trout fry. Wrens have also been seen to catch and eat small goldfish.

(from Bird Life *July/September 1971)*

Treecreeper's mistake

One Sunday, after evensong, I went birdwatching in the churchyard. The church is surrounded by open fields and trees in a semi-rural area. While I was watching a pair of jackdaws high in an elm tree, I felt something at the back of my legs, slowly moving upwards. I turned quickly and in doing so frightened a treecreeper which then flew behind a tree. I was wearing brown trousers and a tweed jacket at the time. I don't know who was more surprised, him or me!

Kevin Warner

(from Bird Life *October/December 1971)*

And another mistake!

One day at my home in Mallow, Co. Cork, I saw a treecreeper sitting on the saddle of my bicycle. The bird flew to the ground and began to climb the wheel. It came to the handlebars and then went along the crossbar and under the saddle, where it stayed for about three minutes.

Michael Moloney

(from Bird Life *April/June 1972)*

In the swim

While on a canoeing trip on the Grand Union Canal at Foxton in Leicestershire, I saw a bird land on the water about 30 or 40 metres in front of me. At first I thought it was a gull, but as I got closer I discovered it was a woodpigeon. When it saw me it moved through the water to the bank, got out and flew away. I have seen woodpigeons in 15 cms of water but never before in water two metres deep.

Christopher Coater

(from Bird Life *April/June 1972)*

Airlift

One day in April I was with my father and a friend on the nature trail at Elsham Hall near Brigg in Lincolnshire. We were passing through an area of damp undergrowth with silver birch, bramble and bracken when we disturbed a woodcock with its young. The parent bird collected one of the young ones between its thighs and took off. Its tail appeared to be curled under, as though it were providing a support for its offspring. The chick was dropped in some bracken nearly 30 metres away. Immediately, the parent bird flew into another clearing 20 metres farther on and trailed a wing as though pretending it was injured. All the time the bird was making an alarm call. We had a quick look in the area where we first saw the bird and we found a second chick. According to my father, this was about a week old.

Howard Burton

It is known that woodcock sometimes carry their young in this way, but few people have seen this happen.

(from Bird Life *July/September 1973)*

Woodcock

S C Brown

continued on page 51

24

A Birdwatcher's Paradise

I woke up. My back ached a little. The firm sand at the top of a Mediterranean beach makes a hard bed! Somewhere above my tent a short-toed lark was singing its abrupt snatches of song, and I knew I had overslept. It was five o'clock.

Behind the tents was a low pebbly dune. The previous evening we had seen the mysterious green light of glow-worms here—cold, still, animal-flamed—but now a pink glow in the east and a cloudless sky told me that we were in for another scorching mid-June day. As I walked over the dune a salt lagoon came into view. Common terns had a colony on an island, and their screams reminded me of the RSPB reserve at Minsmere, Suffolk. A few dozen avocets feeding in the shallows and several black-headed gulls resting on the water could also have been Suffolk birds, but not those six flamingoes, dwarfing the avocets with their extraordinarily long legs that seemed unnecessary as the birds stood in only a few inches of water.

You would never feel heat like this in East Anglia, either. The sun was up now, and I pulled off my T-shirt. It was six o'clock.

Two of the gulls caught my attention. Their heads were completely white, unlike black-headed gulls, all of which have at least a dark mark behind the eye, and most of which sported the full

open-hoods of breeding adults. The beaks looked different, too. I flicked a mosquito off my arm and set up the telescope on its tripod. A few moments later I was looking, for the first time in my life, at slender-billed gulls. A lucky find, this, for they are scarce birds in the Camargue. I hauled my grunting companions from their tents to have a look, while the sun poured its heat over everything. Soon a shimmering haze obscured all but the nearest birds, and I had to put a shirt over my burning back. It was only half past seven.

We were in the south-east corner of the triangle of land called the Camargue, on the south coast of France. The three sides of the triangle are formed by the sea and two rivers: Petit Rhône and the Grand Rhône. It is a large area, 293 square miles in all, and it contains a number of different habitats. Thanks to this diversity, the climate, and the protection offered by the nature reserves, the Camargue boasts a magnificent variety of wildlife. The area is valuable to birds at all times of the year: more than 150,000 ducks winter on the lakes, countless migrants feed and rest here in spring and autumn, and there is a large breeding population.

The Camargue is the delta of the Rhône, which was once an even larger river than it is now. Over many years the sea has gradually retreated, leaving a series of salt-water pools. A map of the area is dominated by water: there are lakes, ponds, swamps and irrigation ditches. The nearer you are to the sea, the saltier the water. The

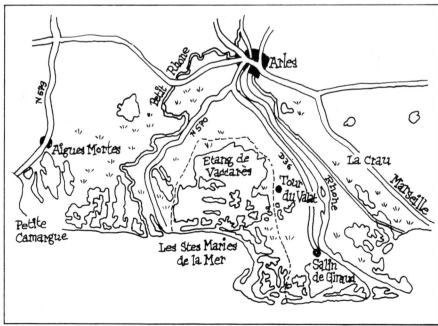

● by John Seymour

Little egrets

G D Plage (Bruce Coleman Ltd)

went, and bee-eaters were incredible colours in the sun.

Into first gear along the world's worst road, grinding around pot-holes, until we came to open water. Common terns fished here, and a moustached warbler perched on a reed, and a pratincole flew right around us, its brown "armpits" catching the sun. We could hear geese somewhere on a distant farm. Another half-mile, and the étang opened right out. There are geese in the middle of the water—not geese at all, but more than 2000 flamingoes, honking, feeding, and revealing startling red and black markings on

heart of the Camargue is a large salt-water lake, the Etang de Vaccarès.

A good way to appreciate the open "lay-out" of the Camargue is to drive right through it as we did, taking several days over the journey. We started from Arles, the nearest large town, and headed south-west along minor roads, past small villages and fields of wheat, with Cetti's warblers singing suddenly and violently from thick hedges, and rollers perching on telegraph wires. Reeds appeared, fringing dry fields and marking the lines of ditches. As a tractor sprayed chemicals over the stumpy vines, a reed warbler sang from a corner of a field and then a nearby great reed warbler began its raucous song. Fan-tailed warblers dipped and "zipped" in their strange song-flight. It was a misty dawn; a night heron flew silently over us as we sipped coffee, crested larks were feeding fledged young on the dry soil beside the road, and a black kite settled coldly on a pylon.

On again, until we were on a rough track overlooking a wide expanse of reeds through which we could see some water. This was the northern edge of the Etang de Vaccarès. Suddenly the Camargue was all around us. Black-winged stilts pursued each other noisily, little egrets and purple herons stood silently over shallow water, gull-billed terns flew past, a coachload of German tourists came, used our telescopes to look at the bulls, and

Night heron

Bernard Rebouleau

Bee-eater

S C Porter (Bruce Coleman Ltd)

their wings as a helicopter put them to flight.

Almost dusk; we had taken all day to travel seven miles and the two Young Ornithologists in our group were almost satiated with new birds! Kentish plovers ran about on the dry sands beside small, shrivelling ponds, and spectacled warblers appeared and disappeared in the shrub. We were near the coast now, back to tarmac and tourists, and the famous white horses were splashing through the salt marsh with tiny children on their backs.

How can you describe the Camargue in a few words, or experience it in a few days? And I have still not mentioned the other superb areas nearby, such as the stoney desert of La Crau, where pin-tailed sandgrouse and black-eared wheatears breed, short-toed eagles hunt for snakes, and the air is warm with the scent of thyme.

Then there is the mountain ridge, les Alpilles, where Dartford warblers flit among the hard leaved bushes and beautiful yellow and orange butterflies, the Provençal species of brimstone, flutter over the rocks.

Egyptian vultures live here, and can also be seen at the foul, fantastic garbage heap at Entressen, where the city of Marseille dumps its rubbish to be blown about by the mistral wind. Join the more adventurous tourist on the top of the Roman aqueduct, le Pont du Gard, lie on your belly to peep over the edge, and you will see rock sparrows nesting among the historic stones.

But the centre of attraction is, understandably, the Camargue —for the time being. Pesticides and fertilisers are soaking into the étangs, wildfowl swallow shot and are poisoned by the lead, wetland is being reclaimed to grow rice, and huge industrial developments are planned nearby. The French Government has proclaimed parts of the Camargue a national reserve, but that only keeps out tourists, not chemicals. It will take more than luck and a change of name to protect this magnificent area for future generations of both bird-watchers and birds.

Flamingoes

Robert Gillmor

How to catch Birds

Who on Earth would spend hundreds of hard-earned pounds on producing a small piece of celluloid with nothing on it but a picture no bigger than a matchbox?

Or spend hour after hour in extremes of weather waiting and waiting for something that hardly ever happens?

Or sit up half the night searching scientific papers for a hint about when a certain bird might be likely to perform a certain rare display?

You've guessed it—a bird photographer.

To hunt a bird with a camera can be the most frustrating, exhausting and infuriating way of spending time. But it can also be thoroughly absorbing, immensely exhilarating and totally satisfying.

I first became involved with it at the age of twelve, when I spent half of a frustrating afternoon trying to get close enough to a flycatcher to make the bird's image in the viewfinder of my box Brownie camera look a little larger than a golf ball at 50 yards. Fortunately my next subject was a mute swan on a nearby lake. I was thrilled to find that even I could bring home a photograph that did some small justice to the grace and splendour of a wild bird.

From then on I became fascinated with the subject. But how could I get a better quality picture of a small bird without spending a fortune on camera equipment?

Soon it became clear that the only way to achieve quality is to get close to the subject. But how do you get so close? There are two methods. Creep up on the subject or get the subject to creep up on you—better still, fly up. This means using two aids: concealment and bait.

If a bird doesn't know you're there it won't be afraid to approach you, and if it has a good reason to come in your direction—

Spotted flycatcher

M D England

with a Camera

for food or water for example—it will be keen to come.

The best place to try this is in your own garden. You already know that to a great tit or a greenfinch in winter a bag of peanuts can be irresistible. And if you're hidden behind a small screen over a nearby window you won't have to wait long before you suddenly experience that thrill of being really close to a wild bird.

In summer, dig up a few worms, put them out on a lawn regularly at the same time for a few days to build up the confidence of your local blackbirds or thrushes and then hide a few feet away.

If the birds don't suspect your presence, they'll be within reach of a good photograph before you have time to realise they are there.

Having overcome the problem of getting close to the birds it is of course vital to have the equipment to take the photograph you're after. I've already hinted that if the bird is large, a swan for instance, you don't need such a big lens as you would if the bird is small. So if you only have a simple cheap camera you won't be able to take on many small birds satisfactorily. There are two main difficulties: a cheap camera will not allow you to change from the normal family

● by Anthony Clay—Former Head of RSPB Film and Photographic Department

snapshot lens to a telephoto lens nor will it have a viewfinder that lets you see exactly what the camera is seeing.

If you want to achieve professional results it really is essential to overcome these two barriers. You must use a camera which will take a variety of lenses and have a facility which allows you to see through the lens when you are lining up the shot. The technical description for a camera with these facilities is "a single lens 35 mm reflex camera with a focal plane or electronic shutter". If you take this description to your local photographic dealer he will tell you what he can supply. Go to a reasonably large dealer—the chances are that he will have a used camera department and this will be a good hunting ground for up-and-coming young professional wildlife photographers. Many a keen young enthusiast has profited by picking up a good used camera cast-off by an amateur who bought the best but never learnt to use it.

Greenfinch

Dr John Woodward

For advanced work you will ideally need a 400 mm telephoto lens—a smaller lens than this will limit your opportunities severely.

A camera of this kind will also have a shutter speed of not less than 1/1000 of a second.

A slower speed than this will be nothing like fast enough to stop the action of a moving small bird.

So, to summarise, learn about birds, work to get close to them and search for good basic equipment. If you follow this simple advice the fascinating world of bird photography will be at your feet.

Mute swan

Dennis Green

Places for Birds

Leighton Moss

Reserves are super places to visit during the summer holidays, but they are more than picnic and play areas. Mike Everett of the RSPB's reserves department explains why we have nature reserves.

As you read this, there will be over 70 RSPB reserves covering over 20,000 hectares of land. These figures look impressive and certainly they show how much we are doing to save places for birds and other wildlife—but when I tell you that they represent less than one-thousandth of all the land in the United Kingdom, you will realise that there is still plenty for us to do. Even if we add together the areas of *all* the nature reserves in the United Kingdom (including those of the Nature Conservancy Council, the county Naturalists' Trusts and so on) we find that the total area set aside for wildlife conservation is less than one-hundredth of the total land area.

Our reserves vary considerably in size and type. Morecambe Bay, in Cumbria, for example, covers about 2400 hectares of tidal mud and saltmarsh, and provides refuge and large feeding areas for tens of thousands of waders in autumn and winter. It is part of the

Loch Garten

Frank Hamilton

Sunset over Morecambe Bay

Michael W Richards

D T Ireland

most important estuary system in Britain for birds and, if a reserve there is to be a success, it must be a large one. The enormous number of birds using the Bay need large areas for feeding and for the several roosting places they use at high tide. The Morecambe Bay reserve is nearly twenty times the size of Leighton Moss, which is right next door to it, but in its own rather different way, the Moss is just as important. About three-quarters of its 130 hectares are reedmarsh and open-water areas,

providing a home not only for hundreds of duck and other waterbirds but also for a large number of reedbed specialists like reedwarblers and water rails. There is also an important bittern population (about nine pairs—there are probably less than 80 in the whole of Britain) and bearded tits, once almost unknown there, have colonised Leighton Moss in the last few years and are increasing in numbers. Reedmarsh is a scarce habitat anywhere, especially in northern England, and Leighton Moss is

● **by Mike Everett**

therefore a very important reserve: just a hundred or so hectares are immensely valuable for the large numbers of birds living and feeding there.

By comparison, some reserves are really tiny—but they too can be of considerable importance. Take Grassholm, for example, an island of only nine hectares off the Pembrokeshire coast, but holding nearly 20,000 pairs of gannets, and fourth largest colony in the world. Coquet Island, off the Northumberland coast, is even smaller (six hectares) and here we have had over 3500 pairs of Arctic, common, roseate and Sandwich terns of four species, including over 1600 pairs of the latter, while the Lamb (a couple of hectares of rock in the Firth of Forth) has had about 200 pairs of cormorants in some years —the only regular colony in that part of Scotland. Tiniest of all is Swan Island, in Northern Ireland, a mere tenth of a hectare, but with a breeding population of between 300 and 500 pairs of terns in recent years. Reserves for breeding seabirds can be very small and yet can still hold large and important populations—important because the British Isles provide nesting areas for a substantial proportion of all the seabirds in the North Atlantic. We have plenty of bigger reserves too with large numbers of seabirds—places such as Bempton Cliffs in Yorkshire, and Handa in Sutherland, or Fowlsheugh, bought for the RSPB by members of the YOC.

I cannot describe all our reserves here, but perhaps mention of a few more will give a good idea of the sort of places we own or manage and the wide range of birds found on them. Scottish reserves include Fetlar, in Shetland, where the snowy owls breed and where other birds include redthroated divers, skuas and whimbrel. There is also Loch Garten, famous not only for its ospreys but also for pine forest and special birds like capercaillies and crested tits. In Northern Ireland there is Castlecaldwell Forest Reserve, whose nesting birds include the common scoter, while in Wales we

Heron

Eric Hosking

have both estuarine and woodland birds at Ynys-hir, on the Dovey estuary, and oak woodland and open hilltops in "kite country" at the Gwenffrwd.

Among the English reserves there is Coombes Valley, in Staffordshire, with its hillside woodland and a stream where you can see both dippers and kingfishers, and the Ouse Washes, Cambridgeshire, well known for the black-tailed godwits breeding there and internationally important for the thousands of ducks and hundreds of Bewick's swans which spend the winter there. Minsmere, in Suffolk, has a variety of different habitats, such as woodland and heathland, and another important reedmarsh, with bitterns and marsh harriers, while its avocet colony is second in size only to the one on nearby Havergate Island. In north Kent we have over 180 pairs

of herons at Northward Hill—the biggest heronry in the UK—and at Arne we are preserving one of the best remnants of Dorset heathland and its highly specialised wildlife, which includes the Dartford warbler.

I think we have every reason to be proud of our reserves and the way in which we and our wardens manage them for birds, but you will remember that I said earlier that we still have a tremendous amount to do. This really boils down to more reserves, but I wonder how many of you know how we decide which areas to go for—or why we normally have 20 or so potential reserves "in the pipeline" at any one time?

In the reserves department we have a good idea where all the best bird places are and we know a great deal about the birds which live in them. Because we have colleagues based as far apart as Shetland and Devon, as well as in Wales and Northern Ireland, we are able to gather up-to-date information from all over Britain. This is added to existing knowledge from records and reports made by various people and organisations over the years. From this mass of information, we can see which areas are "safe" (some are already reserves, while others are not at risk in any way) and which are possibly threatened, so we are able to decide which new reserves we should attempt to secure first. All this gives us the basis of our "Reserves Plan".

Acquiring the land we want can happen in a number of ways. Often we hear that a site becomes available or we ourselves approach the landowner with a view to establishing a reserve over his land. Where we can, we prefer to buy the land, since ownership nearly always gives us the best control over it and the chance to develop it in our way. Land, however, is very expensive and we can only spend so much in any one year (although we can, of course, launch an appeal to raise more money for reserves purchases, like the recent "Save a Place for Birds Appeal" for

Coombes Valley

P Merrin

£1,000,000) so we have to lease land as well. This means we pay a landlord a rent in return for certain rights of occupation and management of his land and often we can spend months, or even years, bargaining until we reach a satisfactory arrangement. But if the terms are arranged properly a leased reserve can be as valuable to conservation as one which we own.

This has been a very brief look at reserves and what they mean. You can learn a lot more from articles in your magazine, *Bird Life,* and from the RSPB magazine, *Birds,* but perhaps an even better way is to visit our reserves and see for yourself. Visiting details are published every year in *Birds* and are always available on receipt of a stamped addressed envelope from the Reserves Department, RSPB, The Lodge, Sandy, Beds. SG19 2DL.

Snowy owl

Bobby Tulloch

LA-C

THE MIGRATION GAME

START Throw a 6 to begin

ENGLISH CHANNEL See special conditions.

Rules

Swallows, like many other British birds, are summer visitors. In autumn they leave Britain and migrate to the warmer climate of South Africa. They must overcome many hazards if they are to complete the long journey.

Play the migration game—two or more players can take part. You need a dice and a counter or ½p piece to use as a marker.

How to play

1. Imagine you are a swallow setting out on your autumn journey. You must wait for fine weather, so throw a 6 before starting. Each player throws in turn.

2. Having thrown a 6, throw again and move on the number of squares indicated. Each square represents about 100 miles of the journey.

3. Follow the instructions in the squares you land on.

4. Many swallows die during the journey. If you are "killed" by a hazard, you must start again, as a "new" bird.

5. There are two "special conditions" squares at sea-crossing points. If you land on one of these, look at the "special conditions" box below.

6. The winner is the first player to arrive in Durban—a journey of 6000 miles.

Board squares

- You find an easy pass through Pyrénées. Go on 1 square.
- Shot by a hunter. Start again.
- Cloud covers sun. Miss a turn while it clears.
- Fog slows your flight. Take 1 off next score.
- MEDITERRANEAN See special conditions.
- Spend time feeding before crossing Atlas Mountains. Miss a turn.
- Wait for good weather to cross Sahara. Throw 6 to move on.
- Good conditions for direct flight. Move on 3 squares.
- Stop and feed at oasis. Miss a turn, but add 2 to next score.
- Sandstorm kills many swallows. Start again.
- Rich feeding on flies near goats of nomads. Go on 2 squares.
- Following wind. Go on 3 squares.
- Bush fire ahead in Nigeria. Make a detour. Go back 2 squares.
- Long flight across Sahel tires you. Take 1 off next score.
- Long flight across desert. Take 1 off next score.
- Drought. Miss turn while looking for water.
- Rest after long desert flight. Miss turn. Take 1 off next score.

Good feeding while you--fly. Go on 2 squares.

Tropical rain storms in Congo Basin delay you. Miss a turn.

Cloudy conditions delay you. Take 1 off next score.

Rich feeding. Miss a turn, but add 2 to your next score.

Swarms of insects easily caught. Go on 2 squares.

Clear fine weather. Go on 2 squares.

Chased by bird of prey. Go back 3 squares.

Rich feeding at Lake Nakuru. Move on 2 squares.

You follow insects around a herd of elephants. Go back 2.

Victoria Falls—head winds slow you. Miss a turn.

Rain storms. Take 1 off next score.

Eaten by bird of prey. Start again.

Danger of over-shooting. Wait until you throw a 6 to finish.

Slowed by worn feathers. Wait to throw a 4 to finish.

Johannesburg—trapped at bird-ringing station. Go back 1 square.

DURBAN You have arrived! 6000 miles completed.

Paula Youens.

Put Life in your Birds

Birds are such lively creatures, so full of energy and movement, yet how often drawings of them appear dull and lifeless! In this article, Dr Eric Ennion, one of today's best-known wildlife artists, gives you some useful hints to help improve your bird sketches.

I believe birds should always be drawn from life, rather than from pictures, photographs, skins or stuffed specimens. Only then will you catch their true shapes, quick actions and liveliness. To me, these are far more important than intricate plumage patterns, invisible at ordinary watching distances, or exact colours which can change with the light and with age.

Sketching birds from life demands more knowledge of their anatomy and behaviour, more patience and practice than just copying from photographs. But, if you love drawing, and are ready to persevere, it is well worthwhile.

Birds in zoos, parks and waterfowl collections are good subjects to begin with. They are used to people, and are often fairly large birds not easily hidden by cover.

You will need a fair-sized sketchbook—I find an A3 Daler layout pad most useful—and some

good quality B or 2B pencils. Learn to draw freely and never be cramped for space or hand movements. Pianists' and typists' fingers move *unseen* swiftly and accurately over the keys. You must learn to draw almost unseen too—your eyes should be kept on the bird.

Choose a resting group and pick a bird in an interesting pose.

Study it carefully and make half a dozen sketches of its head; then of its feet if you can see them. These are its most important features —don't go on until you have them right. *Don't waste time rubbing out:* good draughtsmen should hardly need india-rubbers. Draw it again beside the first one, and again . . . you will succeed in the end.

By then the bird has moved! This is bound to happen. It may have settled down again, or you

take another bird and go on sketching that. So you fill the pages, bits and pieces, good and bad, and here and there a sketch worth saving. I mark these with a tick for future reference: the others can be struck out. Blame them on the bird for moving!

So far you have concentrated upon outline drawing; for, until you have learned to draw quickly

● by Eric Ennion

and accurately, keeping your eye on the bird, no amount of filling-in or colouring will hide mistakes! The next step is to shade-in carefully places where strong shadows or markings suggest it. You may even add a touch of colour. There is no need to do a special drawing —choose one of your best sketches.

You will be wanting to use your colours now in any case. Biros or even crayons may do for odd splashes of colour, but for speed and handiness watercolours have no equal.

Thick water paints like gouache or poster-paints will not give you the softness and delicate colours of birds' plumage in your outdoor sketches; still less will acrylics, oils or pastels. Used in the right way, watercolours are ideal: they must be transparent.

You do not need a paintbox with all its pans of colour and little mixing "dips"; nor a lot of brushes; nor an easel. The lighter you travel, the less there is to lose or forget! For outdoor sketching, speed and simplicity are essential. It is far better to work with a few basic colours and discover the end-

Common Crane

less tints and tones you get by *lightly* mixing them with water on a wide-open palette. I use an old, white enamel plate—*not* a plastic one! The secret is to squeeze little dabs of tube-paints round it below the rim. With waterpot handy, fill your brush and draw down onto the plate. *Mix very loosely,* adding water if wanted, until you see the right shade and strength

Condor

appear—and there you are!

Many watercolour artists only carry half-a-dozen tubes when working out-of-doors, but their lists vary. Mine would be: ultramarine blue, lemon yellow, raw sienna, light red, alizarin crimson, Chinese white.

These colours, plus water and palette, a couple of brushes (say a no. 6 and a no. 8) and some 2B pencils, are all I need—apart from paper, of course. For quick colour sketching like this, a pad of school cartridge paper is ideal; a large bulldog clip stops the pages flapping. An easel is not necessary, though a folding stool is useful.

Catching the bird's correct shape and proportions is more important than its exact colours. Colours change not only with the light, whether the sun is high or low in the sky or in front or behind the bird, but also with age, sex and moult. In painting, I always put a transparent brownish- or bluish-grey "wash" (made by mixing ultramarine and light red) over the darker, shaded parts of the drawing, letting it dry before washing the final colour over the top.

Also, I often use tinted paper, giving the lighter, sunlit parts of the bird a *thin* "wash" of Chinese white and letting it dry. Then,

instead of a flat bird outline, you have a perfectly "modelled" shape ready for its final colouring. Already it looks alive!

Watercolour paper, tinted pale bluish, or buffish greys, can be bought; but for sketching I like old business envelopes, etc. Use the rougher insides (their shiny outsides will not take paint!) and avoid those that have an obvious ridged or criss-cross pattern. With a little ingenuity and Sellotape you can build up a pad of these on a firm cardboard backing—a home-made tear-off drawing book. And always remember—pencil on paper but eye on the bird!

WINGTIP TO WINGTIP

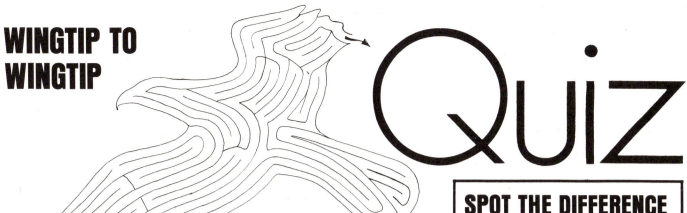

In

QUiZ

Trace the path through the eagle from wingtip to wingtip.

BIRD SQUARE

A	L	L	O	H	A	O	V	E	L	*out*
W	S	T	W	S	G	H	S	T	E	E
C	O	O	S	Y	O	N	N	E	R	I
R	E	H	T	E	R	A	G	O	M	P
W	H	C	T	A	C	C	K	O	A	G
T	I	R	O	A	T	U	C	T	S	E
E	T	H	O	T	S	D	L	I	C	R
H	C	E	N	C	K	R	N	N	D	L
A	T	B	L	A	B	I	E	T	G	O

This square is made from the names of thirteen British birds.

Find a pathway through by moving backwards, forwards, up or down, spelling out the names of the birds. You may not move diagonally. Enter the square on the left edge with a bald-headed bird. Pass through every letter and leave by the 'out' sign at the top right-hand corner.

Here is an example of how the birds are hidden.

O	R	M	O	*out*
C	N	I	R	T
R	O	B	A	N

SPOT THE DIFFERENCE

At first glance these pictures look identical, but the second picture differs from the first in several small points. Can you find all twelve differences?

BITS OF BIRDS

Like weird creatures from a naturalist's nightmare, these birds are a strange mixture of British birds. Can you identify all eight species?

Left-hand bird Tail (1)....................
    Wings and legs (2)..................
    Head and neck (3) ....

Right-hand bird Head (4) ....
    Neck (5) ....
    Body and wing (6) ....
    Feet (7) ....
    Tail (8)..................................

Answers are on page 77

The Fulmar Petrel

David and Katie Urry

Spending the winter at sea the fulmar, or, to give it its proper name, the fulmar petrel, only comes ashore during the breeding season. Now a familiar sight where cliffs are suitable, this bird has become one of the most successful seabirds breeding in Britain today.

The word fulmar comes from the Norse "fu'll" meaning "foul". This is due to the fulmar's habit of squirting up an evil-smelling mixture of regurgitated food on anyone who comes too close to its nest ledge. I can imagine that many a Norseman scaling the breeding cliffs in search of fulmars must have cursed when, on reaching the appropriate ledge, the fulmar squirted its stomach contents over him.

Fulmars are not the most beautiful of birds, but they are masters of flight; using the air currents they can glide for hours with no apparent effort, wings straight and taut, tail slightly angled, obviously in a state of equilibrium. It is the rigid wings when gliding which make the fulmar easily recognisable even to novice birdwatchers. When flying, they use all eddies and gusts of winds to the maximum advantage. I never tire of watching fulmars, wheeling and circling above their breeding cliffs, and I think that in flight they are among the most exhilarating of our native seabirds.

The fulmar's breeding season lasts from May to September, and I urge anyone interested in fulmars to visit one of the many colonies dotted around our coast during this

time of year. The size of the colonies varies considerably; the biggest colonies are on St Kilda where 40,000 pairs breed yearly. The total fulmar population in the British Isles is over 300,000 pairs.

If you visit a colony, you will notice that the young are at different stages of development. Some adults may have small, downy chicks, and others have juveniles nearly ready to leave the ledges, while some may be incubating eggs. Incubation is shared by both sexes and lasts for about 53 days, an unusually long period of time. In fact, fulmars incubate their eggs for longer than any other British bird. You will become absorbed in the comings and goings at the nest sites. You will probably see the parent birds feeding the young fulmars; this is a messy job as not all the regurgitated food goes down the young bird's throat.

Sometimes fulmars will nest near the top of the cliffs and I have often seen birds sitting on eggs just a metre below the top. Being tight sitters, they refuse to move, and this gives you a marvellous opportunity to view these birds at close range, to see the tubular nostrils and darkish-grey back. Often, as you approach, a sitting bird will utter its guttural call, a strange note from deep down in the throat.

As you leave the cliffs, with the birds wheeling and circling overhead and the whole fascinating process of colonial life going on below, you leave, in my opinion, one of our most exciting seabirds— the fulmar petrel.

● **by Kenneth Graham** (YOC Member)

Making a Pond

Have you ever thought of making a garden pond? It is quite simple and the end result can give you and your family many hours of pleasure watching the birds which come to drink or bathe. Birds need water all year round and a pond would be a useful companion to your bird table. Moulds for ponds can be bought from gardening supplies shops, but here are instructions for making a pool using thick polythene or PVC sheeting.

After you have obtained your parents' permission, dig a hole about two metres long and one and a half metres wide. The deepest part should be about 30 cms and the floor should slope gradually to a shallow end. Remove all the sharp stones.

You will need a piece of sheeting large enough to overlap the edges of the pond by about 60 cms on each side. Lay the sheeting in the hole, and secure the overlapping edges with earth, turf and stones. Sprinkle about 10 cms of soil over the base of the pool. Another thin layer of gravel or sand should prevent the water becoming too muddy.

A few aquatic plants can be placed in the earth, while irises around the sides of the pool will help to secure the banks and at the same time add an attractive splash of colour. Fill the pond with water slowly to avoid disturbing the base. Then roll a log or large branch into the water to provide the birds with a good perch.

In a short time you should find that a variety of birds regularly visit your pond and quite possibly it will also attract other wildlife to your garden.

Getting Them Taped

Many years ago I wrote that wildlife sound recording is "the most glorious sport of all" and since then I have never changed my mind. The bird recordist has to pit his wits against his subjects. He has to watch and learn about them; he has to place a microphone in a place where the song will not be too faint or distorted, and he has to battle against the weather and the noise of traffic and aircraft. But at the end of the day there are the rewards—a recording of a song or bit of activity, each a crystallised moment of time.

I made my first bird recording in 1950, using a disc recorder and a standard moving coil or dynamic type of microphone. The necessary equipment was costly and cumbersome, so I experimented with magnetic tape for bird recording and I was soon convinced that it was better. I could carry out recordings with a portable machine, the surface hiss was lower and it was possible to record for up to 43 minutes at a time: a great advantage if the bird song or call was short and only given at long intervals. I could run the tape backwards, clean it of sound and use it again without having to change it. Tape recording also collected more sound than the old disc recorder; more birds could be heard, giving the recording a special depth so that it sounded more "natural".

Today there are many different kinds of tape recorder on the market which have made wildlife recording easier, but in the 1950's a small high quality one was a novelty. I recorded waders massed on the Hilbre Islands in the Dee estuary, brent geese on the Blakeney mudflats in Norfolk, and once waded for three-quarters of a mile into a chest-deep lagoon in the Camargue, southern France, to record flamingos on their nesting island! I also recorded a pair of stone curlews at the RSPB reserve at Minsmere, Suffolk. The sounds included all the alarms, contact and display notes and a conversation between the hen bird and a chick inside the still unbroken shell before it hatched out! While working at Minsmere, I obtained a rich harvest of recordings—the boom of bitterns, the calls of bearded tits and many other birds. In 1964, while directing a BBC film about the wildlife there, I recorded the call of a marsh harrier as the male in its display flight climbed and plunged, tilted and looped the loop over 100 metres above the marsh.

A parabolic reflector is a bowl-shaped device allowing you to record birds at a greater distance and at the nest without disturbing them. It can be a tremendous help in recording birds out on mudflats or in the middle of reservoirs and other large lakes, and in flight. I recorded a cuckoo calling 420 metres away and pink-footed geese at a range of 1000 metres with the help of a metre-wide reflector, but a smaller one can be used with great effect as well. Parabolic reflectors are not the whole answer and should be used only in open situations—not near walls, cliffs or large trees which can be reflecting surfaces. Smaller reflectors tend to act rather poorly with low frequencies, are less directional and pick up less sound energy. However, it was not until I used reflectors that I was able to record swifts screaming in flight because there had always been a drop in pitch with a fixed, open microphone.

The nearer you are to a bird the better the result but your microphone must not be too close or the sound may distort. The opportunities increase if you lengthen the microphone cable, but this can add noise and distortion to your recording. Dynamic microphones give a good response over the most important frequencies; they are strong and have a low impedance which allows them to pass energy over quite long lengths of cable. To save having to run out enormous lengths of cable I experimented with radio transmitters and receivers and broadcast the songs and calls coming into the microphone by radio link to a tape recorder some distance away. We recorded white-fronted geese at Slimbridge with a cableless gap of 1000 metres between the reflector and the recorder, and later we increased this distance to a mile for snow bunting calls at Cley in Norfolk. I had great fun making sound recordings by radio-link of migrating birds as they passed the gallery of the old Dungeness lighthouse in Kent. One night hundreds of goldcrests came in and some alighted on the rails of the gallery. A few even perched on my shoulders and among them was a magnificent firecrest!

Over the years I have visited some of the most exciting places and regions in my quest for new recordings of birds. But birds have not been my only concern. I have also tape-recorded red deer in the Grampians and fallow and Sika deer in the New Forest, coypus in Norfolk, grey squirrels in Cheshire and I spent a thousand hours over four years capturing the vocabulary of the badger—my favourite British mammal. I have also recorded frogs and toads, hawkmoths and beetles, water boatmen and leaf-cutting bees, and fish underwater.

Although there are many aids to sound recording, the original need for patience still exists. Time spent studying subjects beforehand is never wasted. By mapping their territories and song posts the information I gather helps me to decide where to place the microphones.

Early morning is generally the best time for recording birds. In spring and summer territorial singers will sing more loudly then, the air is often still, and there are fewer man-made noises. I cannot possibly count the number of dawns I have seen during my bird-watching life! For me it really is the best time of the day, when nature seems most confiding.

Since I began recording twenty-seven years ago, tape recorders have become much cheaper and cassettes have also appeared. It is possible to make quite a range of recordings on these home recorders covering a range of different species as well. Some of the cheaper recorders may carry inbuilt distortion or "wow" and "flutter" caused by the irregular movement of the tape over the magnetic heads. This can result in trills and "wobbles" in the recorded bird sounds. Dirty parts and not enough maintenance can cause these effects as well. So practice with the recorder is needed as well as patience. It is possible to walk about a wood or garden and make recordings on a cassette recorder but as you take the matter more seriously you may find that you need a longer cable and more professional equipment. To obtain the best results you need quality equipment able to cope with the wide frequency range of some bird sounds, but there is no reason why you should not start with less ambitious gear provided you know its capabilities. Cassettes of bird song are available commercially and last year I produced an album for BBC Records of two discs and two cassettes of garden and woodland birds which are also sold by the RSPB.

Some professional bird recordists have used cassette tapes to lure birds closer to their professional equipment. I have only once done this, when I recorded firecrests in an English wood, but on the whole I see certain dangers in this practice, when used too frequently—dangers of confusing resident birds, even forcing them to desert, and this is something that should be avoided at all costs.

In a recent edition of *Audubon*, an American conservation magazine, it was made clear that bird-watchers in the United States were using cassette tapes to lure shy and rare birds into view. Birds were deserting or being attacked by predators listening out for the return call. In some regions one tape recorder called to another with no birds in between!

One recent development is stereo wildlife recording, which can give an extra dimension to the sound. This involves the doubling-up of techniques—a split reflector with two microphones, a special stereo recorder and so on. It is expensive, but the results are often exciting and dramatic. One summer I was invited to join an expedition to the Camargue to make stereo recordings of the wildlife. We obtained the first stereo recordings of many birds and animals and were very pleased with a colony of flamingos, black-winged stilts yelping over their damp marsh, warblers in full song, a mixed colony of night herons, little and cattle egrets squawking in a small wood and tree frogs filling the evening air with their rattling chorus. However, many mono recordings are still the best in their field and are likely to remain so for a long time to come.

Many of the recordings that I have made over the years have been for the BBC. I used to play them over at slow speed and discovered, for example, that the nightjar sings 1900 notes to the minute and the grasshopper warbler 1400 *double* notes to the minute. Many sonograms, or sound pictures, have also been made which show both the pitch and length of each call or song burst and these can be studied at leisure. Copies of recordings are also kept at the British Library of Wildlife Sounds in South Kensington.

Of all the many and varied things that I have done in my very enjoyable life, the recording of wildlife sounds was without doubt the most rewarding. But I have always put the welfare of the birds first. Birds must not be disturbed during the breeding season and they should not be harried with microphones or tape recordings. It is still possible to make recordings with care and patience, keeping for us sounds that will bring pleasure and perhaps instruction for the rest of our lives.

Stone curlews

S C Porter

1978 Competition

Identify the birds on page 46 and win a pair of binoculars

The month of May, somewhere in the south of England, and the countryside is full of birds . . . Can you identify all 30 species on the following page?

The competition is divided into three age-groups: one for children aged nine and under, one for 10 to 12-year-olds and one for the 13s and over. There is a pair of Zeiss Jena Jenoptem binoculars for the winner of each group. (The age groupings are taken as from 1 January 1978.)

Send your answers on a postcard to RSPB Bird Life Annual Competition, Purnell Books, Berkshire House, Queen Street, Maidenhead, Berkshire SL6 1NF by 31 March 1978.

Only one entry per person, please, and don't forget to include your name, age on 1st January 1976 and address. The editor's decision is final.

Long-eared Owls

Frank V Blackburn

The City Dwellers

House sparrows

City birds have learnt to live alongside Man. They can survive where other species find it impossible to do so. Just try to imagine guillemots in Glasgow, buzzards in Birmingham or crossbills in Cardiff, and you realise that the sparrows and pigeons there are rather special. How do they manage so well?

If you have ever stood in a city square and fed the pigeons at your feet, or thrown crusts to sparrows round a park bench, you will think of one reason straight away. In towns there is plenty of food for birds which are not too fussy. Certainly not sprats for guillemots or cones for crossbills, but bread and scraps wherever people keep bird tables, share their lunch with the birds, or just drop crumbs. In school playgrounds after break, under the tables of an open-air cafe and poking about in the litter bins, birds clean up the left-overs. They find grain too. When city traffic meant horse-drawn cabs and coaches, there was corn to be picked from the gutters, or even stolen from the horses' nosebags. Now it is taken from warehouses, flour mills, animal-food factories, and bakeries. In some places pigeons, especially, can be an expensive nuisance.

Not all food is provided by people. Even in the most built-up areas there are patches where tough plants grow, supplying seeds and insects for the birds. These green places are most important in the nesting season when worms, flies and caterpillars supply the soft protein that growing birds need. In parks, squares and gardens, and in accidental sanctuaries like development sites, car parks, and railway banks, a surprising variety of birds manage to find a living. Starlings, blackbirds, robins, blue tits and woodpigeons are there, with perhaps dunnocks, thrushes, and chaffinches too. Large open spaces like the Royal Parks in London are home for many others. On an island in Regent's Park boating lake there is a heronry. Great crested grebes nest nearby and also on the Serpentine in Hyde Park. Many wild

Jane J Miller

● by Keith Noble

Feral pigeon

David and Katie Urry

49

A–D

ducks come each winter to join the tame collection in St James'. A few very keen birdwatchers who visit their park nearly every day can actually see a hundred species in a year!

From a bird's-eye view, the tall buildings of our cities might look like rocky cliffs, with ledges to perch on and dark corners and nooks for nesting. Town pigeons are descended from wild rock doves which live in coastal caves and crevices, so they find built-up areas ideal. They usually prefer older buildings as the ornate stonework provides good roosting sites with holes and gaps leading into safe places to nest. Churches and railway stations are popular with pigeons. Often there are starlings too, and in several cities thousands

not nest right in the heart of our cities, probably because the air is not clean enough to support sufficient flying insects for them to feed on. Two other birds nest on buildings and eat insects. One, the pied wagtail, is quite common and well known; the other, the black redstart, is a rarity. Strangely, its favourite haunts are gasworks and power stations!

Many cities are built on rivers and grew rich though the trade the rivers brought to them. They were the first places away from the coast to be visited by gulls, which are now so common inland that it may seem strange that they are quite recent arrivals. They did not reach the docks and rubbish dumps, parks and reservoirs, much before the start of the century. Now they

hunt out every scrap as if they were making up for lost time. Other water birds have also increased. As more and more reservoirs and gravel pits have been dug and flooded, they have been found by thousands of ducks which leave northern Europe to spend the winter here and they also find their way to town ponds and lakes, bringing pleasure to city birdwatchers. If you are one of them, why not make a special study of the parts round your home? As many birds nest in a typical area of town houses and gardens as in the same area of mixed woodland. See how many species you can find, and by noting where they are and what they eat, try to find out how they live so well with people.

Starlings

S C Porter

of them fly in from their feeding places each evening to pack the ledges and enjoy a warmer night than they would in the country. City streets are sheltered and all the warmth from their traffic and industry, from centrally-heated offices, shops and homes, raises the temperature a degree or two.

Kestrels, the YOC symbol, can sometimes be seen in cities —they have bred on churches, law courts, flats and museums, and at least one tower block has a nest-site specially made for them. In suburban roofs swifts raise families, and another summer visitor, the house martin, builds its mud nest under the eaves. They do

50

continued from page 24

Outlook

Dennis Green

Long-tailed tit

A sleepy bird

While bird-watching near Stanmore, we saw three long-tailed tits feeding in hawthorn scrub. As we approached within one metre of the birds, one of them put its head under its wing, shut its eyes and fell asleep! We called gently. It opened its eyes, looked at us, then fell asleep again. The other two birds fluttered near it, calling and apparently disturbed as if the bird were one of their young. This, however, seems unlikely as the bird was fully fledged, and it was too early in the year for this season's young to be flying and feeding themselves.

Christopher Kightley

It is very difficult to give any explanation for this behaviour; the bird may have been showing some of the symptoms of shock and the other birds were worried by its strange behaviour.
(from Bird Life *July/September 1972)*

Collecting straw

Near where I live is a small rookery and opposite our house is a field. During February the farmer manured the field and the rooks took advantage of this sudden abundance of straw for their nests. A few days later there was a fall of snow, but this did not deter the rooks. They landed on the snow-covered field, rolled on their backs and flicked away the snow with their tails. The birds then picked up the straw, flew round the wood and returned to their nests.

Michael Christdon

(from Bird Life *July/September 1971)*

Rook smoke-bathing

In September I was looking out of the window of Hollins School, Lancashire, when I saw a rook fly to the chimney. The rook then began to hold its wings out over the smoke. It was raining at the time. Although it flew away it returned several times and went through the same actions.

Nigel McHugh

It is thought that smoke-bathing helps rid the plumage of lice and fleas. Rooks are one of the commonest birds to be seen smoke-bathing, but the reason for this is not fully understood.
(from Bird Life *April/June 1973)*

Strange behaviour of Coot

On a trip to Tring Reservoirs in July, I saw some coots behaving in a strange way. While one stood very upright on the bank facing out across the water, the other swam about in front of it. However, each time it passed in front of the standing bird, it jumped right out of the water as if it was about to dive, but did not do so. This happened about 12 times. A third bird stood on the bank nearby.

David Evans

E L Turner in her book Broadland Birds *describes how coots, upon approaching another bird's territory, throw themselves out of the water and beat upon the surface with both feet for several seconds. Although this is not quite what David saw, it may be a variation on the display for the same purpose.*
(from Bird Life *October/December 1972)*

Garden visitor

One day in August in my garden in Cheadle, Cheshire, I spotted an unusual bird hopping around the back lawn. It was roughly the size of a fully-grown song thrush. The head and neck of the bird were light brown in colour, almost identical to those of a song thrush; the breast was half speckled with dark brown and fawn, and half with dark brown and black. The rest of the body and the tail were black, similar to those of a male blackbird. The bird has often been seen with another bird with similar markings.

Christine Brooks

Birds fitting this description probably puzzle many people when they first see them. The birds which Christine saw were almost certainly juvenile male blackbirds which were moulting from their juvenile plumage into the black plumage of the adult males. Before they moult they resemble song thrushes and this is very confusing for beginner birdwatchers.
(from Bird Life *January/March 1973)*

Most often seen as a ghostly-white shape flying silently in the gathering dusk, the barn owl, with its heart-shaped face and sequin-spangled mantle, is easy to recognise. It tends to haunt old buildings and farms, as in this case, when a pair chose to nest in an orange-box which had been slightly modified and placed on a beam at the top of a Dutch barn.

These pictures were taken by Dennis Green, who spent five weeks photographing the owls from a hide erected on scaffolding.

Photos 1 & 2 A six-week-old youngster peers cautiously out of the box.

No 3 Wing-stretching exercise.

No 4 One of the parents hurries into the box carrying food—a short-tailed vole.

No 5 A shy look from a young bird as it preens.

Home
Sweet
Home

Club Members' Cartoons

ISN'T IT EXCITING THEY'RE GOING TO NEST IN *OUR* GARDEN.

Jonathan Poole (10), 38 Meadow Road, Stonehouse, Gloucestershire.

Barbara Moffat (14), 12 Woodland Avenue, Widnes, Cheshire.

James Bennett (15), 27 Ladybarn Road, Manchester, M14 6WN.

"PLEASE DON'T DO THAT

THIS HUMAN IS INTERESTING. EVERY TIME WE COME NEAR, IT BURIES IT'S HEAD...

"NO PESKY VARMINT GOING TO GET MY THIS YE

K. Reader (16), 36 Long Park, Amersham, Buckinghamshire.

Byron Edwards (12), 26 Oaklands Road, Bridgend, Glamorganshire.

David Fotheringham (10), 19 Kirk Brae, Kincardine-on-Forth, Fife.

James Bennett (15), 27 Ladybarn Road, Manchester, M14 6WN.

King of the Birds

The golden eagle is still the prize bird for most birdwatchers visiting Scotland. No matter how famous the ospreys or snowy owls have become, these "big birds" are still firm favourites.

Golden eagles are not so uncommon as many people suppose, but they certainly present a challenge to the average observer. Spotting them often requires patience and persistence; finding them usually means avoiding the more populated areas and, finally, they are easily confused with the buzzard.

But before we talk about "eagle spotting" and identification, here are some basic facts. All golden eagles bear the scientific name *Aquila chrysaetos*—"*Aquila*" is the Latin word for an eagle, and "*chrysaetos*" is a Latinised form of the Greek "*khrusaetos*", derived from two Greek words, "*khrusos*" meaning gold, and "*aetos*" meaning eagle.

In Britain, the golden eagle is mainly found in the Highlands and many of the Western Isles of Scotland, but there are a few pairs in south-west Scotland and one pair breeds in the Lake District. They are essentially birds of mountain country, although in some areas they occur on moors and quite low hills and many occasionally nest on coastal cliffs.

The exact number of British pairs is not known, but is probably more than 250 and may even be 300. They are more numerous here than in any other part of Europe and it seems likely that Scotland holds a quarter of the whole European population.

Each pair covers an area of between 11,000 and 18,000 acres in search of food. Within this area they nest either on a crag or in a tree (usually a Scots pine), having alternate sites which they use in different years. Some pairs may nest only on cliffs or in trees; some do both. The nests, or eyries (pronounced eyeries), are huge structures, especially those in trees—one nest was found that had been used so many times it was recorded as almost five metres deep!

The nests are built of sticks, branches and often heather, lined with woodrush, grasses or similar plants, and frequently decorated with ferns and rowan sprigs. As a rule, two eggs (sometimes one, more rarely three) are laid in the second half of March. They are large and whitish, marked with very variable amounts of reddish-brown blotches. In a typical clutch, one egg is often well-marked, while the other is almost white. The young hatch after about six weeks and are covered at first in white down. They stay in the nest for 10 to 12 weeks before taking their first flight. In western areas, where natural prey tends to be scarce, it is usual for only one young bird to survive. But in the east, where food is more plentiful, it is common for two young to be raised successfully.

RSPB surveys over the last ten years have shown that eagles are holding their own and not decreasing as we once thought. However, many are still persecuted by shepherds and gamekeepers, while

Walter E Higham

even more are disturbed by other human activities, including photography and birdwatching. Some are robbed by unscrupulous egg-collectors. So the RSPB still needs to keep a close watch on their welfare and, as far as we can, we maintain strict secrecy about their nest-sites.

While they can and do kill with a spectacular dive from a height and sometimes catch other birds on the wing, golden eagles normally hunt slowly and methodically, often for hours on end, coursing low over the ground, then killing their prey with a short burst of speed or a sudden dive. They take a wide range of medium-sized animals and birds, but rabbits, hares, grouse and ptarmigan are their favourite prey. In areas where natural prey is scarce, sheep and deer carrion are important, especially in winter. Lambs are only rarely killed and most are in fact picked up as carrion.

Occasionally, I have seen golden eagles from main roads, as well as from trains and steamers, but have usually had better luck walking in the hills away from roads and people. In spite of their great size (about 75–88 cm long with a wingspan of about 185–240 cm), they can be very hard to see against a hillside, so watch for them along the horizon and the

Dennis Green

tops of hills and mountain slopes.

They are visible to the naked eye over a mile away. At such long range they may look very dark or even black, but their long-winged outline and slow, majestic flight will help in identification. Very often ravens, crows or other birds can be seen "mobbing" them and this gives you a useful size-comparison.

Probably every "golden eagle" seen sitting on a telegraph pole is

in fact a buzzard, and most large birds of prey you see soaring over valleys, woods and hillsides are also buzzards. At close range identifying eagles is not difficult, but when the bird is farther away problems arise and size alone is not a safe guide. Remember that golden eagles are uniformly coloured below—they lack the markings under the wings which are so characteristic of most buzzards. Eagles also have relatively longer wings and tails, their heads protrude more obviously. Their bills are much larger and they only rarely call in flight. If you see an adult eagle from above, you may find its wing-coverts are noticeably paler than its flight feathers and you will probably also see the pale, straw-coloured crown and nape (which otherwise may not be so obvious as pictures in your bird book suggest). Young eagles have obvious white flashes in mid-wing and white bases to their dark-tipped tails—features which often show up at very long range.

If you come to Scotland to see a golden eagle, don't expect to spot one straight away—you may be lucky, of course, but to be sure of success you will probably have to spend some time searching. Remember, they are very shy (contrary to popular opinion, they will not attack you at the nest!). So if you do find a nest—come away quickly. ● **by Mike Everett**

John Marchington

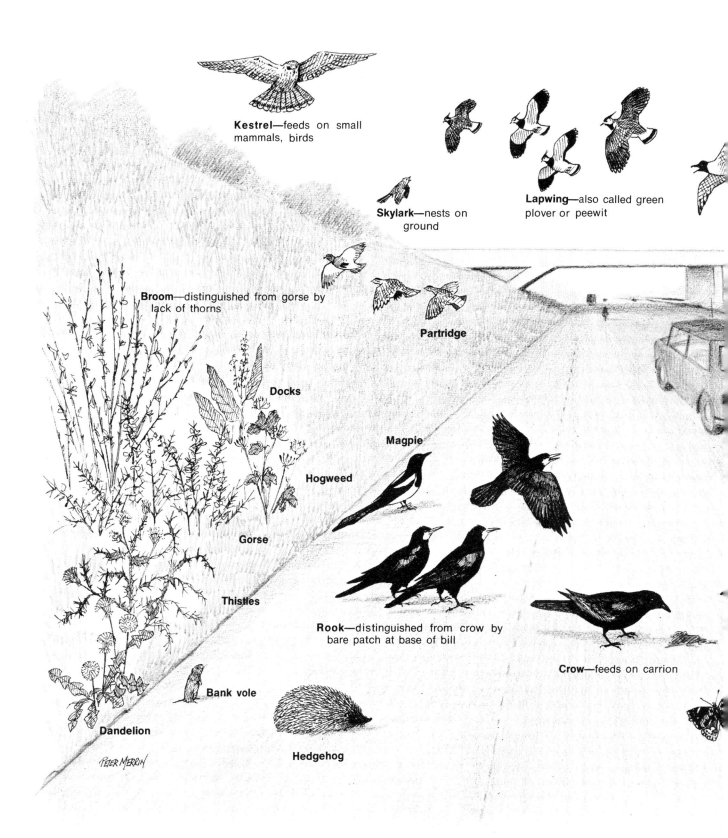

Kestrel—feeds on small mammals, birds

Skylark—nests on ground

Lapwing—also called green plover or peewit

Broom—distinguished from gorse by lack of thorns

Partridge

Docks

Magpie

Hogweed

Gorse

Thistles

Rook—distinguished from crow by bare patch at base of bill

Crow—feeds on carrion

Bank vole

Dandelion

Hedgehog

PETER MERRIN

Motorways

Pheasant—cock

Painted lady butterfly
—feeds on thistles.

Do you find car journeys boring, or are they an exciting chance to watch the countryside? Next time you travel on a motorway, look out of the car to see how some wildlife has adapted to this relatively new, man-made habitat.

You may see a kestrel hovering above the verge. Head into the wind, tail fanned wide, wings beating swiftly, its keen eyes search for bank voles. Watch the roadside —you will probably see rooks, crows, and possibly a magpie. Members of the crow family, the opportunists of the bird world, are quick to spot an easy meal and often eat dead animals lying at the roadside. For more information about their feeding habits, read the article on pages 60 and 61.

You are likely to notice black-headed gulls feeding on nearby farmland, while the lapwing is also conspicuous with its spectacular display flight, a pied tumbling shape rolling and wheeling above the fields.

Pheasants and partridges too are familiar, but skylarks are less easy to recognise. They are the small brown birds that fly from the verge, flashing white edges to their tails and wings.

Many plants grow on motorway verges. Amongst the commonest are docks, hogweed and dandelions, while gorse and broom are found on sandy banks. Thistles are also common, and are a favourite food of the delicately marked painted lady butterfly.

Animal casualties are a sad feature of motorways, although proportionately fewer birds are killed on motorways than other roads. Curiously, hedgehogs' behaviour seems to have changed in recent years. They used to curl up when approached by a car, but now they often keep running, or return to the side. Perhaps this is a form of evolution—those with a tendency to run survived to breed.

Deer can be a problem, but can be deterred fairly successfully by mirrors that reflect car's headlights. Badgers are not so easily swayed, though on the M53, in Cheshire, one positive step has been to provide a badger crossing under the carriage-ways. These and other measures, such as careful landscaping and planting of motorway verges, and thoughtful management, should enable more wildlife to live side by side with man.

Adult rook

E A Janes

Motorway Feast

Rooks and crows feeding beside motorways are a common sight, but have you noticed how their numbers vary at different times of the year?

When I first realised this, it seemed strange that even if there were plenty of quiet, relatively safe fields in which to feed, rooks should use noisy motorways. Before looking at why the numbers of rooks should vary, I thought I should make sure that the numbers really did change: it might have been that I travelled on more motorways during certain months.

Obviously, I needed help to record the times when the birds were seen. Therefore, I prepared some forms and enlisted the aid of a variety of observers, from young people to the motorway police in Wiltshire.

When the forms were returned, the information showed that rooks and crows seem to be drawn to motorways when the verges are moist in spring and, to a lesser extent, in autumn. During dry weather or frost very few rooks or crows are seen on motorways.

Now, what could cause these variations? Almost certainly the rooks and crows were attracted to motorways for food. Therefore it had to be a food that was affected by weather, particularly dryness and cold, and it had to be something that rooks ate. Of all the animal and vegetable matter eaten by rooks, the most likely candidate was the earthworm.

Why should earthworms be easier to obtain on the verge of a motorway than on the verge of any other road? Possibly the worms were sensitive to vibrations caused by traffic. If so, then were there more vibrations on motorways than on other roads?

To find out, I called on the help of an inventive colleague, who made a "semi-seismograph" from a generator, record-player, amplifier and an oscilloscope! With this piece of equipment we measured vibrations on different types of road. That the biggest vibrations occur on motorways, especially on hills, quickly became obvious. We now needed to know the effect of vibrations on worms.

In a mechanical engineering laboratory at the North-East London Polytechnic, my colleague, Dr Peter Spence, and I experimented to discover earthworms' reactions to vibrations under various conditions.

Generally, the wetter the soil, the faster worms come to the surface when vibrated. However, the

Adult rooks
E A Janes

60

Carrion crow

R J Chandler

reactions are not clear-cut—one species will not surface at all, while in certain soils, such as sand and peat, no worms surface. Worms seem to be most sensitive to low-frequency vibrations like those produced by traffic on motorways or foot stamping. Our laboratory tests enabled us to predict the conditions under which earthworms would come to the surface, thus becoming prey for rooks and crows.

Stamping will bring worms to the surface. Scientists studying the behaviour of herring gulls and lapwings have noticed how these birds will stamp to bring worms to the surface of wet meadows. The results of our investigations into the behaviour of rooks and crows seem to show that these cunning birds allow man's motor vehicles to do their stamping for them and vibrate their food to the surface.

● by Roger K Tabor

Charting The Unexplored

Today we accept research as vital to our way of life, a means of increasing our understanding and knowledge of our surroundings. But this was not so in the past, when scientists and researchers were often looked upon as eccentrics. Charles Darwin, an early naturalist, was the subject of much scorn and controversy when he published his book, *Origin of Species*, which suggested that Man and apes shared a common ancestry. In the following story we trace his fascinating round-the-world voyage which helped him formulate many of his theories on evolution.

CHARLES DARWIN AS A YOUNG BOY SPENT MOST OF HIS TIME CATCHING BEETLES FOR HIS COLLECTION.

WHILE ATTENDING UNIVERSITY, HE WAS ASKED TO JOIN THE SHIP H.M.S 'BEAGLE' CAPTAINED BY ROBERT FITZROY AS ITS NATURALIST.

AFTER FIVE ATTEMPTS, THE 'BEAGLE' EVENTUALLY LEFT DEVONPORT ON 27 DECEMBER 1831, HEADING FOR THE CAPE VERDE ISLANDS IN THE MID-ATLANTIC.

HE'LL NEVER MAKE THE TRIP, HE'S ALWAYS ILL.

THE SHIP SAILED ON TO BAHIA BLANCA, IN SOUTH AMERICA. WHILE THERE, DARWIN DISCOVERED THE REMAINS OF PREHISTORIC ANIMALS.

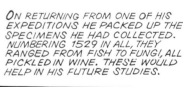

ON RETURNING FROM ONE OF HIS EXPEDITIONS HE PACKED UP THE SPECIMENS HE HAD COLLECTED. NUMBERING 1529 IN ALL, THEY RANGED FROM FISH TO FUNGI, ALL PICKLED IN WINE. THESE WOULD HELP IN HIS FUTURE STUDIES.

AT THIS STAGE CHARLES BEGAN DOUBTING THE STORY OF THE CREATION IN THE BIBLE, WHICH UNTIL THEN HAD BEEN UNDISPUTED. THIS SUBJECT BECAME AN ARGUING POINT FOR MANY A LONG NIGHT BETWEEN DARWIN AND FITZROY.

IN MAY 1833 THE 'BEAGLE' PUT DARWIN ASHORE AT MALDONDANA TO CARRY OUT HIS SURVEYS.

EL CARMEN WAS THE NEXT PORT OF CALL AND DARWIN'S PLAN WAS TO RIDE ACROSS 600 MILES OF UNEXPLORED PAMPAS TO BUENOS AIRES, CALLING AT BAHIA BLANCA EN ROUTE.

THEIR WAY AT FIRST WAS ACROSS THE DESERT. HERE THEY FOUND AN ASTONISHING AMOUNT OF WILDLIFE. DARWIN TOOK SPECIAL INTEREST IN THE FLIGHTLESS RHEA.

DID IT EVER FLY?

DARWIN ALSO ENCOUNTERED MANY OTHER STRANGE ANIMALS, INCLUDING A SMALL BLACK AND VERMILION TOAD, WHICH, MUCH TO HIS SURPRISE, ALMOST DROWNED WHEN HE PUT IT IN WATER.

ON ARRIVAL AT BUENOS AIRES HE SENT A FURTHER 200 SKINS OF BIRDS AND ANIMALS HOME AND REQUESTED MORE EQUIPMENT.

AFTER A STAY OF FOUR MONTHS, THE 'BEAGLE' LEFT BUENOS AIRES AT THE END OF 1833.

IN MARCH 1834, DARWIN LANDED IN THE FALKLAND ISLANDS AND IMMEDIATELY WENT TO WORK.

THE SHIP RAN AGROUND IN PORT DESIRE. DARWIN AND FITZROY TOOK THE CHANCE TO EXPLORE THE LAND BEYOND RIO SANTA CRUZ.

DARWIN WASTED NO TIME IN VISITING THE ANDES.

SAILING AGAIN, THIS TIME AROUND THE TIERRA DEL FUEGO, ON OCCASION THE RIGGING FROZE, AND THE DECKS WERE COVERED WITH SNOW. ON 22 JULY 1834 THE SHIP ARRIVED AT VALPARAISO. DARWIN'S PACKAGES WERE WAITING FOR HIM. HE WENT TO STAY WITH A FRIEND.

HE MADE A STARTLING DISCOVERY IN THE MOUNTAINS: A BED OF FOSSILISED SEASHELLS.

THESE ROCKS MUST ONCE HAVE BEEN BELOW SEA LEVEL.

HOW DID THIS, AND OTHER CREATURES, GET HERE ON THIS ISLAND?

WHILE ON THE ISLAND, DARWIN DISCOVERED AN UNKNOWN SPECIES OF FOX. IT WAS SO INTERESTED IN THE GOINGS-ON OF THE SHIP THAT DARWIN WAS ABLE TO CREEP UP BEHIND IT AND HIT IT OVER THE HEAD WITH HIS HAMMER.

THE SHIP SAILED ON, VISITING THE MANY SMALL PORTS AROUND THE ISLAND OF CILOË, ENABLING DARWIN TO STUDY THE SEALS.

ON JANUARY 1835, WHILE IN THE BAY OF SAN CARLOS, THE WHOLE CREW WATCHED A VOLCANO ERUPTING A HUNDRED MILES AWAY.

THE SHIP SET SAIL AGAIN, AND HEADED FOR THE ENCHANTED ISLES, THE GALAPAGOS ISLANDS, WITH THEIR ABUNDANT WILDLIFE. A GROUP OF SAILORS WENT ASHORE WHERE THEY ENCOUNTERED THE ISLANDS' IGUANAS AND GIANT TORTOISES.

THIS ONE'S STILL ALIVE— IT'S BEEN DOWN AN HOUR!

I WONDER HOW IT CAN SURVIVE SO LONG?

DARWIN BEGAN A STUDY OF THE TORTOISES. AT THIS TIME, WHEN SO LITTLE WAS KNOWN ABOUT WILDLIFE, SCIENTISTS NOTED EVERY OBSERVATION. DARWIN ALSO CARRIED OUT EXPERIMENTS WITH THE MARINE IGUANAS. ONE WAS THROWN INTO THE SEA, WEIGHTED. AFTER AN HOUR IT WAS STILL ALIVE AND KICKING.

HE TOOK SPECIAL NOTICE OF THE BIRDS, WHICH WERE SO TAME THEY WOULD DRINK FROM A PITCHER OF WATER HELD IN THE HAND.

ON BOARD, DARWIN BEGAN TO SORT THROUGH THE MANY SPECIMENS OF PLANTS AND OTHER WILDLIFE HE HAD FOUND ON THE GALAPAGOS ISLANDS. THEN HE REALISED THAT ALMOST ALL OF THEM WERE UNIQUE SPECIES. MORE QUESTIONS AROSE IN HIS MIND.
HE STUDIED THE FINCHES ON THE VARIOUS ISLANDS AND NOTICED THEIR DIFFERENT BEAKS: THERE WERE SEED-EATERS, INSECT-EATERS AND NECTAR-EATERS. LATER IN DARWIN'S LIFE, THIS OBSERVATION WAS TO PLAY A MAJOR PART IN HIS THEORY OF EVOLUTION.

THEY MUST HAVE ADAPTED TO THE DIFFERENT FOOD FOUND ON EACH ISLAND.

AFTER JUST OVER A MONTH, DARWIN RELUCTANTLY LEFT THE ISLANDS. THEY WERE NOW HOMEWARD BOUND. HE FOUND THE REMAINING PORTS OF CALL VERY INTERESTING, AS THEY STOPPED AT TAHITI, NEW ZEALAND, AND AUSTRALIA, BUT HE FOUND HIS MAIN INTERESTS LAY IN THE SOUTH AMERICAN COUNTRIES.

THE HOMESTEADS OF NEW ZEALAND RESEMBLED THOSE OF ENGLAND AND MADE HIM FEEL VERY HOME-SICK.

BY THE SPRING OF 1836, THE 'BEAGLE' WAS PUSHING HER WAY THROUGH THE INDIAN OCEAN, CALLING AT THE COCOS ISLANDS, WHERE DARWIN WATCHED THE COCONUT-EATING CRABS.

HOW WELL THEY HAVE ADAPTED TO THEIR ENVIRONMENT!

DUE TO BAD WEATHER AT THE CAPE OF GOOD HOPE, THE SHIP WAS DELAYED, AND IT WOULD NOW BE OCTOBER BEFORE THE 'BEAGLE' RETURNED TO ENGLAND.

FITZROY TOLD THE CREW THAT TO COMPLETE HIS MAPPING SURVEY PROPERLY THEY MUST RETURN BY WAY OF BAHIA BLANCA.

THE 'BEAGLE' SAILS INTO FALMOUTH.

THE VOYAGE OF THE 'BEAGLE'.

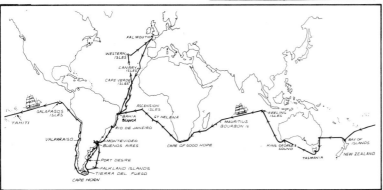

HOWEVER, THEY STAYED ONLY A FEW DAYS AT BAHIA BLANCA AND ARRIVED BACK IN ENGLAND ON 20 OCTOBER 1836. THEY HAD BEEN TRAVELLING FOR NEARLY FIVE YEARS.
DUE TO ILL-HEALTH, DARWIN WAS NEVER TO SAIL AGAIN. BUT THE DISCOVERIES HE MADE DURING THIS VOYAGE ON THE 'BEAGLE' LED HIM TO WRITE HIS CONTROVERSIAL PAPER ON EVOLUTION, WHICH CAUSED UPROAR IN SOCIETY. TODAY, DARWIN IS REGARDED AS THE MAIN INFLUENCE ON THE CHANGE OF OPINION ABOUT ON THE CREATION OF LIFE.

LA–E

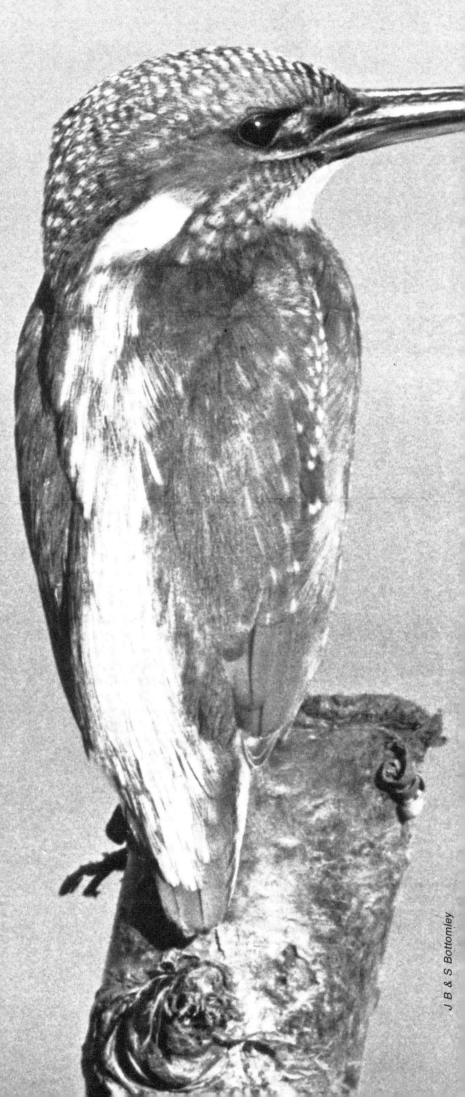

When I first moved to Suffolk, I didn't realise I lived in an ornithologists' paradise. There is a variety of habitats within a mile of my house—farmland, both deciduous and coniferous woodland, and a river. The river is no more than two metres wide, very shallow, but with deep, slow-moving water in some places. Where the river has burst its banks in winter, areas of marshland and reedbeds have formed, providing havens for reed buntings and sedge warblers. Since I have lived here I have recorded 70 different species of birds.

I first became interested in kingfishers when, while out fishing, I found a nest. I was too late to watch the actual nest-building as the eggs were already being incubated, but I decided to study the birds' behaviour.

As the kingfishers approached the nest entrance, they let out a piercing whistle which sounded like an express train. The birds only whistled when they were actually coming to the nest—if they were flying past, they remained silent. However, when excited or angry they whistled twice in quick succession.

Sometimes I watched the king-

Dennis Green

Ronald Thompson

Project Kingfisher

fishers fishing. They rarely hunted close to the nest, but it was more usual to see them as I walked along the river bank. They killed their prey by bashing it against a branch. The birds then swallowed the fish head first, so as not to choke on the gills and bones.

The eggs hatched eight days after I found the nest; I saw the shells floating in the water. For the first week one of the adults stayed with the young, then both parents collected food. An evil-smelling green slime of excreta and rotting fish dripped from the nest-hole; young kingfishers, unlike certain other nestlings, do not produce their droppings in special faecal sacs.

After about 16 days the young kingfishers ventured from the nest and perched on the branches nearby. Their feathers were still in their waxy sheaths. However, as soon as the young birds were fully fledged, their parents left them.

During the winter I did not see the kingfishers very often. The adults became very aggressive towards other birds and chased them out of their territory, even attacking their offspring.

The next year, in mid-April, I heard a commotion coming from a pool about ten metres downstream from the old nest. It turned out to be kingfishers nest-building. The birds took it in turns to fly at the bank and dig with their beaks and

feet. When the first hole was quite long, they suddenly started digging another tunnel next to the original, but they soon gave this up, returning to the original nesting-burrow. After about two weeks I hoped that the female might be laying. Unhappily, my worst fears were confirmed—a rat had driven the birds out.

The burrow was very near the surface and was uncovered the following September when the field was ploughed. The nesting-chamber was only 15 centimetres below the surface and was about 15 centimetres square. The floor was carpeted with fish-bones. The whole tunnel measured 86 centimetres in length.

● **by Philip Woollen** (YOC Member)

What a Hoot!

A do-it-yourself papier-mâché owl money-box

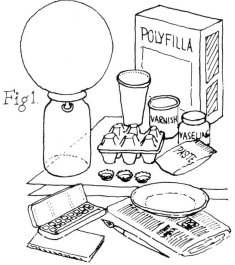

Fig 1.

Materials

Balloon	Newspaper
Vaseline	Jam-jar
Shallow dish	Wallpaper paste
Paper pulp egg-boxes	Piece of strong cardboard
Waxed paper	Small bucket
3 metal bottle-tops	Strong glue
Emulsion paint or Polyfilla	½-pint cream carton
Varnish	Coloured paints

Method

Blow up balloon to size of owl required and completely cover with Vaseline to prevent paper from sticking. Balance in jam-jar with tied end inside jar (fig 1). Mix wallpaper paste with water and pour into the shallow dish. Tear up newspaper into approximately 2 cm by 25 cm lengths.

Dip each paper strip into paste and run your fingers down the strip to

Fig 2.

remove excess (fig 2). Place paper strips over the balloon, smoothing out air bubbles, until it is completely covered. Overlap the edges of the strips and fill any gaps with small pieces of paper, but leave tied end free.

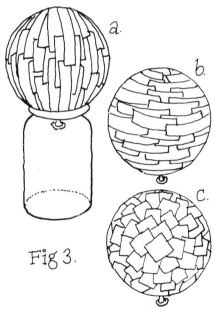

Fig 3.

The *first paper layer* is made of strips of newspaper running over the balloon (fig 3a). The *second layer* is made from strips running round the balloon (fig 3b); the *third layer* from strips over the balloon as in the first layer. The *fourth layer*—tear strips into 2 cm by 2 cm squares and completely cover the balloon (fig 3c). The *fifth layer* is the same as the first layer, the *sixth layer* the same as the second.

Layers of newspaper

1st layer: strips direction (a)
2nd layer: strips direction (b)
3rd layer: strips direction (a)
4th layer: squares (c)
5th layer: strips direction (a)
6th layer: strips direction (b)

When you have applied all the layers, lightly pat the balloon all over; this will remove any small air bubbles and make sure that the paper is well stuck down. The strength of the finished shell depends on the careful application of *each* piece of paper in each layer.

Place the coated balloon, still balanced on its jam-jar, in a warm place such as the airing cupboard. Leave for 24 hours or longer, until hard. Test by gently tapping. When the shell is dry, release the balloon by pricking with a pin or untying —remember to hold on to the balloon as the air rushes out. Remove the remains from the shell and return to the airing cupboard for a further 24 hours.

Meanwhile, cut out the feet from a piece of stiff cardboard (fig 4a), making certain the circular part of the feet is large enough to cover the area left round the tied end of the balloon. Cover both sides of the cardboard and the outer surface of the cream carton with newspaper layers 1 and 2. Dry in the airing cupboard on waxed paper to prevent sticking (many cereal packets contain suitable paper). When dry, glue base of carton to feet and strengthen with strips of paper (fig 4b). Leave to stick with a heavy weight on top (fig 4c).

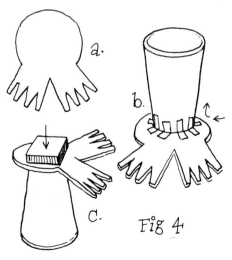

Fig 4

When both the paper shell and the feet are completely dry, it is time to model the ears, eyes, beak, back, wings and talons with papier-mâché.

Papier-mâché

Tear up the paper-pulp egg boxes into very small pieces. Put into a small bucket or basin and add boiling water and washing-up liquid (younger readers should ask an adult to do this for them). Leave to soak for 24 hours, stirring occasionally. The next day squeeze out all the water and rub or crumble the pulp between your fingers. Add sufficient wallpaper paste until you can roll the pulp into a sausage shape without it cracking.

Now you can start modelling. Small pieces of triangular-shaped card help with the shaping of the ears. Fix eyes—metal bottle-tops —to the shell with a piece of pulp. Shape wings, cover back and front with a thin layer of papier-mâché, pushing your fingers into the pulp to make the feather patterns. Model feet with rolls of pulp. Leave for several days to dry.

When the papier-mâché layer is hard, cut a slit between the ears (younger readers should again ask an adult to do this). Use a very sharp knife and carefully cut a slit large enough for a 50p piece.

Paint the body and feet with light-coloured emulsion or, better still, Polyfilla mixed to a creamy consistency. Allow to dry and paint the owl in bold colours. A final coat of varnish will protect your coloured surface. Place the body over the feet and your owl is complete.

A Birdwatcher's Calendar

JULY

Start a holiday notebook. Keep a daily log for the whole of your holiday.

Migrant waders move through Britain and Ireland —any wet areas are worth visiting.

Young birds independent of their parents but not yet in adult plumage can be difficult to identify.

AUGUST

Start a list on summer migrants and note the dates on which you see them. Eventually you will build up a list of "last dates" on which birds are seen.

The countryside is quiet as little song is to be heard. Many songbirds are renewing their feathers and ducks lose their colourful plumage.

Many small birds start to migrate. Among the first are swifts and cuckoos.

SEPTEMBER

Clean out your nestbox and repair it if necessary as small birds may roost in it during the winter.

More summer migrants leave and swallows line up on telegraph wires.

Many unusual birds to be seen at the coast and migrant seabirds move south.

OCTOBER

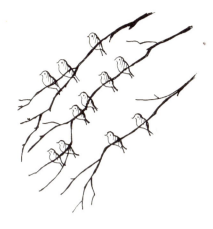

Listen after dark for high-pitched "seeip" of red-wings migrating. These, like many other species, migrate at night when there are fewer predators. Listen, too, for owls.

Thrushes, especially red-wings and fieldfares, are attracted by berries and fallen fruit.

Many birds starting to gather together in flocks, even birds which fought to defend territories during the summer.

NOVEMBER

Start feeding the birds in your garden.

The flocks of geese start to build up in numbers.

Big winter roosts of birds such as starlings and rooks are easier to find.

DECEMBER

Remember to renew your YOC membership for next year and buy the next *Bird Life* annual!

Rubbish tips provide winter food for gulls, both inland and near the coast.

Wildfowl numbers on inland waters increase and whooper and Bewick's swans may be seen.

A Bird in

By the fireside, slipper-footed and relaxed in the deepest armchair, I watch the clock which meaninglessly ticks its way towards too late. Time, the darkness and the window-clawing, midwinter rainstorms mean little, for I can be anywhere outside, in any time, season or circumstance which my mind remembers or imagines.

Another log on the fire, and I can, for instance, be out at dawn, a frost-gripped morning when the grass is plated with crystals and crunches underfoot. The hare, ears flattened to protect his back from the sharp starlight, bolts from his fence-side form and streaks a hundred yards before stopping, curious. There are no guns or dogs —only me, harmlessly walking. The hare has time to flop a silhouetted ear and look. Then it slowly ambles away, along one of the runs which map and contain its hare-brained life.

Only the finches are fully awake, alerted by the hunger which cold can induce in a bird. While dawn is a suspicion of red through the eastern pines, greenfinches, chaffinches and linnets in thousands are pouring into the mustard-field to gorge on the seeds. Finches, like bird-shaped clusters of fruit in the trees, are tinkling their ice-calls into the mustard-plants, swirling like smoke from the flame-coloured mustard and settling until the whole field is alive with hidden twittering. A sparrowhawk sweeps deftly over the wall in a predatory glide, and the finches burst from cover and swirl again or pitch back into the trees. If I fold myself back into the wallside and wait, I may see a hen-harrier come floating across the field, flapping and wing-walking at mustard-top level, ready to twist its great wings in a grasping fall on a bird or rabbit.

Another rain-gust on the window, and I can see the farm track below this field late one autumn afternoon. A sparrowhawk shoots from the moulting oaks into a flock of finches exploding the birds around it. Then, over the hillbrow, the harrier leisurely draws itself into a winged snarl and tilts into the sparrowhawk. One lean talon hits the hawk, which squeals like a struck mouse and dashes off in panic. Having asserted itself, the harrier regally drifts back over the hill.

The fire falls in a shower of sparks. Between placing another log and thinking of bedtime I can be with barn owls, beating backwards and forwards along the sapling spruces, weaving steadily between the tree-stems. They are unreal creatures, trailing spindly, down-covered legs with talons like hooks, landing on tree stumps among bracken and ferns, and straining their great black eyes into the semi-darkness of winter dusk. A rustle behind me, a suggestion of a footfall, and two roe deer walk quietly into a clearing less than a tree-fall's distance from where I sit. Buck and doe, nuzzling at bramble-leaves and lichen. I hardly breathe: I am a tree-trunk, a shadow, or a big, silvery-coloured barn owl, inoffensive to the sight, hearing or scent of a pair of deer. They walk by me, unafraid, and the white patches of their rumps melt into the shadows between the trees.

I stretch and yawn. I listen to the wind-wrecked trees in the rainy dark, and am half in love with my fireside and comfortable human condition, which allows me to imagine a last venture to the marshside at evening. Teal chirrup in the creeks, mallards cackle and splash, and a flight of wigeon goes whistling over. What seems at first like the distant barking of dogs draws nearer and grows musical, becomes greylag geese in a thousand-strong skein coming marshwards to roost. The calls become louder, goose-shapes plummet out of the dusk and splash into the nearby water. For minutes they come, and all the world is geese, wing-beats and wild calling and web-splashing deafeningly down.

When all the geese are at rest and their calls are peaceful, I sneak away homewards to the reality of my own midnight roost.

72

● by Philip Coxon

the Mind

Michèle.

Splash down!

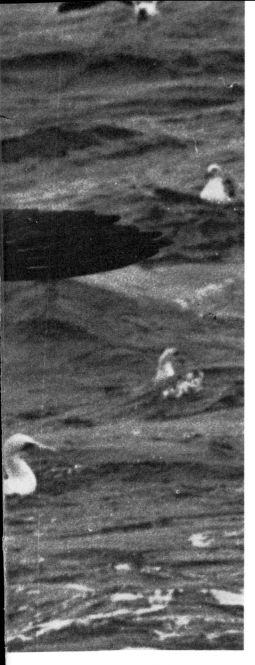

Over 70 per cent of the total world population of gannets breed on the coasts of the British Isles. There are two RSPB reserves with gannetries: Grassholm, which has between 15,000 and 20,000 pairs, and Bempton Cliffs, with about 100 pairs.

These photographs by Anthony Bomford show the gannet's spectacular, spear-like dive.

When my mother was young, a very long time ago, people used to go about the streets of London singing out: "Chickweed and groundsel, for your singing *birdies.*" Singing birdies, mostly canaries I expect, were in many homes, but why was it worth someone's while to bring in bundles of weeds from the country to sell around the streets? Because most of the cage birds, including the canaries, were finches and finches love the seeds of chickweed and groundsel, common wild plants which most gardeners nowadays pull up and burn or put on the compost heap. But what a pity, when once these plants could fetch money for their value as food for finches!

Look in any cage-bird book and it will tell you about wild plants as cage-bird food and medicine too. Obviously, what is good for cage-birds is good for wild ones, so why not keep a corner of your garden for useful seed-bearing wild plants? The following are recommended and you may know some of them already:

Groundsel
Chickweed
Shepherd's purse
Knapweed
Burdock
Thistle
Betony
Fumitory
Sow thistle
Coltsfoot
Dandelion
Teasel
Knotgrass
Docks
Seeding grasses

You won't need to plant most of them—they will come by themselves, and you may enjoy trying to identify them when they first appear. Some parents may look thoughtful at the idea of a weedy corner, others may welcome it as one part of the garden which won't need weeding! Mothers who enjoy flower arranging will approve of the burdocks and teasels which can be used dried for that purpose, after you have shaken out the seed.

Besides the list of weeds, many flowering garden plants produce seed for the birds and some of these are: Michaelmas daisy, cosmos, sunflower and gaillardia. Leave some of the flowers to die off so that seed heads will form.

Why buy wild bird seed when you can grow your own?

Food for Finches

● by Dorothy Rook

The Young Ornithologists' Club Offers Adventure, Fun and Discovery

What does it mean to be a member of the YOC?

Your own magazine

Bird Life is sent free to members six times a year. Full of interesting articles and photographs in colour, it is a must for all young birdwatchers. Regular features in each issue include competitions, projects, and a list of members who wish to make contact with others.

Outings

A special scheme gives YOC members a network, throughout Britain, of adult birdwatchers who are ready to take them on local outings. Trips are also arranged to RSPB reserves.

Holiday courses

YOC courses, held throughout Britain, are not confined to just birds and birdwatching. Many courses combine other activities as well.

Answers

Spot the Difference

Changes in picture 2 are as follows: 1. Extra bird on roof, 2. Tree shape changed, 3. Extra chimney, 4. Extra nail in table, 5. Hook missing under table, 6. Robin's ring missing, 7. More food in front of blackbird, 8. More spots on thrush, 9. Extra bird flying in, 10. Only one tit on nut bag, 11. Extra tit on coconut, 12. Grain of table leg changed.

Bits of Birds

1. Pintail, 2. Redshank, 3. Bittern, 4. Golden eagle, 5. Mute swan, 6. Partridge, 7. Coot, 8. Black grouse.

Bird Square

Coot, Swallow, Shag, Oystercatcher, Whitethroat, Stonechat, Blackbird, Linnet, Goldcrest, Cuckoo, Gannet, Shoveler, Magpie.

YOC Individual Membership £2.00

for anyone aged 15 years or under

First names _____

(Block capitals)

Surname _____

Address _____

_____

_____

Date and year of birth _____

_____

If you would like a YOC metal badge (in addition to your arm badge) please tick here and enclose an additional 30p. ☐

Fill in or copy out the correct section above and send the completed form with your subscription to **YOC, The Lodge, Sandy, Bedfordshire, SG19 2DL.**

YOC Family Membership £2.45

for *any* number of brothers and sisters aged 15 years and under who share one copy of *Bird Life*

First names and dates of birth

(Block capitals)

_____

_____

Surname _____

Address _____

_____

_____

Boy or girl to whom correspondence should be addressed

_____

If you would like YOC metal badges (in addition to your arm badges) please state number required here and enclose additional 25p for each badge. ☐